(A letter to my grandchildren)

Dear Tina, Michael and Kiyo,

As your grandmother, I wish you all the best in the years ahead. You have been blessed with a loving family, good education and sound character.

When I was growing up Mama (my mother) often said to me "Be a Good Life Traveler." And Papa's words of wisdom were, "Be Strong in Mind, Body and Spirit."

My parents were born in Japan in the late 1800s. Life was different then. My life compared to theirs was a vast improvement and you will find your lives will be much richer and better than ours.

Today, as an octogenarian, I feel blessed with my life. My gift to you is my story and I trust you will add to it for your descendants.

Love,
Grandma

Papa Said, "Be Strong"

Kiyo Jean Kariya

Chapter I

My Childhood and Early History

In 1876, my paternal grandfather Kozaburo Ito was fired…as a samurai warrior. The same year across the great Pacific Ocean, Alexander Graham Bell received a patent for the telephone and America celebrated her 100th birthday. But in Japan, my grandfather and thousands of fellow samurais were "released from service" as the Emperor took control of the land from the then-ruling shoguns who subsequently dismissed their legions of loyal warriors.

I never knew my grandfather. The only image of him I recall was a small brown photograph of him and grandmother Take on the Buddhist altar in my parents' house. My father told us little of his own dad although he did take pride in the fact that his parents had very strong teeth with no cavities and were able to read small print newspaper without eyeglasses even in their old age.

My name is Kiyo (Jean) Ito Kariya. I am the mother of three sons (Steven, Scott and Kent) and three grandchildren (Christine, Michael and Kiyo). I live in Maryland and I am writing this autobiography so that my grandchildren, their children and theirs will know about their heritage. I think this is very important and if I were speaking to them now, I would tell them this:

I was born in Oakland, California but my parents were born and lived in Japan before immigrating to this country. Of course, the ancestry of my grandchildren doesn't begin with me or even with my parents but I can relate our family's history as far as what was told to me. That starts with my father's father.

My grandfather, Kozaburo Ito, was born on October 13, 1842 and was a samurai warrior in the Fujiwara clan in Ise, Japan, about 70 miles southeast of Kyoto. I do not know when he became a samurai but he was in the last generation of that warrior class. 1868 was the year of the great turnover – the Meiji Restoration, when the shogun rule of 250 years yielded to the Imperial Rule of the Emperor. In the turmoil of the return-to-the-emperor system, he was relieved of his duty. Facing a bleak future he traveled north to Miyagi prefecture nearly 200 miles northeast of Tokyo and became a farmer.

Grandfather Ito took a strong interest in the national political movement and was a keen admirer of a young activist, Ryoma Sakamoto, who was inspired by the United States ideal, where "all men are created equal." Ryoma sought to modernize Japan so it could compete with the technologically advanced western world which Commodore Perry rather firmly introduced to the then insular and feudal Japanese people. He thought so highly of Sakamoto's spirit, conviction and ideals that he named his second son after Ryoma using the same kanji (meaning *tatsu* or dragon). The local pronunciation of those kanji, though, was "Ryuzaburo."

Thus, thoughtfully named Ryuzaburo Ito was born on July 14, 1883, the 15th year of Emperor Meiji's reign. The Japanese people in that transformative era were highly receptive to the growing modern concept of "the pursuit of individual aspiration." Now referred to as the Progressive Era (late 1890s to 1920s) many Japanese went abroad as tradesmen, students, laborers and adventure seekers.

Ryuzaburo, who I'll henceforth refer to as Papa, at age 22 embraced these popular ideals and sailed on  the Japanese vessel, **Aki Maru** from Yokohama to Seattle, Washington in 1907. He then travelled south to San Francisco where he brushed up on his English at a local high school to prepare for education on a higher level. He learned that in Florida students could work and thus, earn their way through college. So he traveled cross country there journeying metaphorically and literally from the East to the far East (of the United States). He attended and graduated from Ruskin College, just south of Tampa. He continued his studies at the University of Florida and later earned his M.A. in Biology from Stetson University in 1920. While studying, he worked as waiter, dishwasher and janitor to pay for his tuition.

During the summer breaks he fulfilled his love for travel by journeying to forty of the then forty-eight states. Observant and cooperative, but not intimate with racial nuances, he once boarded a public bus in the South. Noting the whites sat up front and Negroes in the rear he quickly sat in the back with the other dark-skinned riders as he himself was well tanned. The bus driver stared at him through the rear view mirror and yelled out, "Hey, you in the back! Get up front where you belong!" Papa, despite being yelled at, felt good about moving to the front as the view was better and the seats less crowded. He applied this experience when he came across segregated drinking fountains and chose the one for whites.

In college, he satisfied his intellectual curiosity by studying astronomy, political science, law, theology, logic and biology. Papa was a diligent and well-behaved student; when the professor had to leave the class he would say, "Ito, take over." In those days, the equivalent of A+ was AA which appeared frequently on Papa's report cards. After seven years of college and graduate school in Florida, he traveled west and settled in San Francisco.

The racial discrimination Papa observed in the South was not directed at Orientals, the commonly-accepted, now-derogatory term, for Asians back then. But, that wasn't true on the West Coast. Employment was scarce and "yellow-skinned" immigrants were seen as lowly and tolerated for menial functions. In southern California it was not unusual for young, college-educated Asian men to work in fruit stands or become gardeners. Times were hard and a job was a job.

Papa started a subsidiary of the Maryland Casualty Insurance Company with Mr. Nakabayashi, a Japanese immigrant like himself, who had just graduated from Stanford University. Together, they sold insurance policies to Japanese immigrant families. Mr. Nakabayashi worked in San Francisco and Papa worked across the bay in Oakland. Their clients were the non-English speaking Japanese in the Bay Area.

Selling insurance was not scholarly Papa's ideal occupation. But in the 1920s the Japanese were restricted by the Exclusion Act and were not able to pursue employment of their choice. If given the opportunity, he probably would have gone into the academic field. Nonetheless, selling insurance was a useful livelihood. He could work from home. And it enabled him to help the non-English-speaking Japanese gradually acclimate to American living. In addition, the Alameda County Court House appointed him an official interpreter (Japanese/English) at court hearings.

My mother, Kane Hirawaki, was born on January 26, 1895, 12 years after Papa was born, in a poverty stricken outskirt of Tokyo. In her teens she responded to an ad for a nanny. Qualifications specified an "alert, healthy young lady who was good with children and willing to travel abroad." Her family and friends thought Kane would be ideal for the job. She applied for the job (which was to work in the household of a

Japanese diplomat soon to be sent abroad) and was hired.

In 1912, at the age of 16, Kane accompanied diplomat Consul General Oyama and family, aboard the **S.S. Tenyo Maru** sailing the Pacific Ocean bound for San Francisco. One of the anecdotes from her first ocean voyage was about the use of the American-style toilet. In those days in Japan everyone squatted over a hole dug in the ground. Sitting directly on the toilet and having bare skin touch the receptacle seemed unspeakably unsanitary. So she climbed onto the strange contraption and squatted on top of the toilet seat. During the rough voyage, she recalled it was "very uncomfortable and scary."

The Oyama household consisted of the couple and their three children (two sons and a daughter) plus a skilled but temperamental chef. The household spoke only Japanese so the Oyamas arranged for an English tutor for the nanny and chef to learn English. Mama studied diligently and learned to read, write and converse on a limited scale.

Coming from a poor class, Mama was anxious to learn not only English but proper etiquette to be worthy of an employee of the Consul General's household. Living in this refined environment, she learned proper manners, elevated language and cuisine cooking. Years later when we were growing up, Mama would introduce us to epicurean dishes she learned in the Oyama household like tongue, pig's feet and oxtail...dishes that, despite her urgings, we really weren't able to, well, appreciate.

When Mr. Oyama's term appointment was up, he and Mrs. Oyama felt that Kane would be happier staying in America rather than returning to her poverty-stricken neighborhood in Tokyo. Since she was of marriageable age, they arranged for a *baishakunin* (go-betweener) to find her a suitable husband. Accordingly, Kane Hirawaki was introduced to Ryuzaburo Ito.

Finding no strong objections on either side, consented to marriage.

Consul General and Mrs. Oyama hosted the marriage at their residence on May 3, 1924. From a surviving photograph, it was indeed an elegant wedding. Mama was beautiful in the traditional white gown and Papa was handsome in his tuxedo with white bowtie. They were a striking couple and honeymooned in Yosemite National Park.

They settled across the San Francisco Bay in Oakland where I was born on September 28, 1925 followed by my younger sisters Masa born on Dec. 6, 1926, Yone born June 18, 1929 and brother Shigeru born Jan. 8, 1932. We enjoyed a happy childhood speaking Japanese at home and English at school, once we started kindergarten.

In Oakland, my parents purchased a two-story house with a small bungalow in the back. Since my parents were non-citizens they were prohibited from owning land in California according to the Alien Land Law of 1913. The property was registered under my name, as I was an American-born citizen and their oldest child. Some forty years later, the McCarren Act of 1954 finally permitted Japanese to apply for citizenship with all rights and privileges. The house with its second floor and the small house in the back yielded welcome income from renters.

We lived in a Japanese community in the outskirts of downtown Oakland. Our neighbors had names like Kanda, Harada, Tanaka, Dakuzaku and Kawamoto. Their professions were journalist, insurance, garage mechanic, food peddler, gardener and domestic. These immigrants all hailed from distant Japan far away from loved ones. But like immigrants to America before us and after us, we found community and fellowship with others like us and became one happy family.

There was a 12-year age difference between my parents. Though Papa was far more educated in a wide variety of subjects, Mama had much better common sense. Moreover, she knew how to get along with people and was loved by all. She was a terrific cook; at pot luck parties her food always ran out first. These ethnic parties usually ended up with a songfest and Mama was the star singer. It's a shame that neither I, Yone or Shig inherited her musical talent.

On the other hand, Papa was a born scholar. He read voraciously and his memory was incredible. He possessed an amazing recall of historical dates and was nicknamed the "walking encyclopedia." Here again, it's too bad none of us inherited Papa's intellectual talent.

Back in the 1920s midwives delivered newborns using sanitary but primitive methods. Pregnant Japanese women during labor didn't have the benefit of ether or pain killers. When I was born, Mama was expected to *gaman* to bear or endure pain as they had done during the samurai days. My delivery was particularly long and excruciating; Mama told me she endured strong pains on and off for 16 hours. She stuffed small towel in her mouth to bite on, and mightily squeezed and throttled her bed's headboard bars to endure the difficult labor. She was a petite lady, under 5 foot and I weighed a whopping 9 lbs. at birth. Every time she reminisced about the ordeal I felt guilty and apologized. "Mama,

I'm so sorry I caused you so much grief," I would say tearfully. A generation later when I was delivering my own children the young mothers bedding beside me in the maternity ward would yell and scream, cursing their husbands for their miseries. And, I thought of Mama suffering silently with me.

Most Asians prefer sons, and the Japanese are no exception. After fathering three daughters, Papa who normally abhorred and ridiculed superstitions wanted a son so badly that he dressed his last daughter in boy's clothing hoping to break the female trend. So, my little sister, Yone, was made to wear pants. (In retrospect, it is a miracle that she suffered no ill consequence, growing up to be a well-balanced, good-natured young woman with no complex. In later years, she was the only college graduate amongst the kids.) Anyhow, Papa's wacky cross-dressing scheme seemed to work. On January 8, 1932 the long-awaited son, Shigeru, was finally born.

In celebration of brother Shigeru's birth, we planted a cherry tree in our front garden and every spring the beautiful pink blossoms perked up our home as well as the entire neighborhood. My parents, sisters and I adored our young brother and denied him nothing which ended up eventually spoiling him, in my opinion.

The 1930's were Depression years; Herbert Hoover was president and the stock market had crashed not once, but several times. The high cost of feeding and clothing four children was not easy. To save money, Papa bought secondhand shoes at the Salvation Army. He would resole these worn-out shoes in his basement workshop before handing them over to us to wear. With newly nailed ¼" cow leather soles, they looked fine but noisily squeaked with each step. Much to my mortification, my classmates seized on the opportunity to loudly tease me whenever I and my new squeaky shoes happened upon them. I went home crying and begged Papa buy me new shoes. He, however, came up with a different remedy -- horsehair. Down in his shop he pried off the new leather sole, inserted horsehair and nailed the soles back on. To my amazement, it worked. So back to school I went in my newly repaired, now silenced shoes.

When the stock market crashed in 1929 ushering in the Great Depression, I was four so I recall very little. In those days significant news was spread by paperboys. They would interrupt the silence of our normally quiet neighborhood by shouting "EXTRA, EXTRA - - READ ALL ABOUT IT!" People would run outside with their pennies and buy the latest edition. The headline was often about some bankrupt Wall Street investors jumping out of tall buildings to their deaths. The rich were suffering. Meanwhile, the poor were queuing up at soup kitchens and sleeping in alleys. Fortunately, Papa had a job and we had a home. I thought how lucky we were to be neither rich nor poor but in the middle – just right.

With her common sense and kind ways, Mama became the unofficial doctor/nurse for the neighborhood and was called upon to care for the sick. Her favorite remedy was mustard plaster which she claimed would lower fever. And, miraculously, it often did. Papa with his English-speaking skills was asked to translate/interpret world and local news as well as assist in filing neighbors' income tax returns. Among friends everything was gratis but come January 1st (New Years) we were showered with gifts of 100 lbs. sacks of rice, large wooden kegs of *shoyu*, miso and bottles of sake – staples of Japanese cooking.

Growing up, we walked everywhere – to public school, library, church, language school, friends' homes, grocery shopping, clothes shopping and to view the annual downtown parades. Papa actually had a car, a Ford Model T, but it was used only for business, summer vacations and special trips.

A special trip might cater to Papa's fascination with astronomy. In our kitchen hung a large calendar with the listing of the various moon phases. Often on nights of a full moon, we would pile into Papa's black jalopy and head for the Chabot Observatory nestled atop the Oakland hills. Through the huge telescopic lens we observed the moon in all its glory. Papa had studied astronomy in college so he tried explaining lunar and planetary concepts but most of it was over my head. Little did I know then that during my lifetime man would walk on the moon.

For exercise and entertainment we spent a good deal of time playing outdoors. Popular games then were: hopscotch, jump rope, hide and seek and roller skating. This was before TV so our indoor entertainment was the radio. We were fans of programs like: **Grand Central Station, The Shadow, The Lone Ranger, Amos & Andy, Fibber McGee & Molly,** etc. This was the time when child actress Shirley Temple was all the rage. There were Shirley Temple dolls, mugs, paper doll cutouts, clothes, anything marketable. I remember wanting a curly-haired, big-cheeked Shirley Temple doll more than anything in my life so I timidly asked Mama if she would buy me one. Mama replied, ever so sweetly, "You really can't play with a doll that expensive. They are decorative and to be admired from afar. You will have more fun making clothes for your Woolworth dolls. You can take it to bed with you without worrying about messing up her golden curls." How true! I learned early in life to be practical rather than be a dreamer.

Like other Japanese families with immigrant parents, we spoke only Japanese at home. When my sisters and I had disagreements we argued in English and Mama would calmly tell us to "argue in *nihongo* (Japanese)." Then, when Mama wasn't around, we would continue our oral battles in English.

Mama told us repeatedly that we were blessed growing up in two cultures (American and Japanese) and to take the best of the two cultures and mold ourselves into a respectable person. She often talked of life's hardships and counseled us to be cheerful and a good traveler in life's journey. She also stressed that money wasn't everything; that kindness, tact and diplomacy were important character traits we should cultivate.

I attended Lincoln Elementary School (K-9) where our classmates were like the United Nations (Chinese, Japanese, Korean, Spanish, Greek, Irish and Jewish). Since most of the parents were immigrants, we were all bilingualists and many of us attended ethnic language schools after public schools. My siblings and I attended Wanto Gakuyen (Bay Area Japanese Language School) from first grade to the upper grades until 1942. There we learned to read, write and converse in the Japanese language. We attended language school every day of the week plus Saturdays at the teacher's home.

My father subscribed to monthly children's magazines from Japan to strengthen our Japanese. The postman would deliver a bundle of the periodicals tied with hairy twine in umpteen knots. Papa would not allow us to cut the string so we had to untie each knot. It taught us patience and economy; to this day I can untie most knots.

One time, after we got our public school report cards, a Caucasian classmate bragged to me how her father rewarded her good grades with a $5 bill. I told Papa this and hinted, "Actually, I got *better* grades." He said nothing. Irked, I sassily pushed further, "...so don't I get *something*?" He looked directly at me and replied, "For doing what? Mama and I give you a good home, three nutritious meals, a place to study and a set of the most recent encyclopedia. Sounds like a good trade-off, don't you think?" That shut me up.

During the ten or more years of studying Japanese, I had many teachers. Most of them simply followed the textbook lessons but a few deviated and went beyond the mundane chapters. One teacher taught us *kendo* (Japanese fencing using bamboo swords). Another young teacher fresh from Japan thought we should know Emperor Meiji's Imperial Mandate, commonly known as *Chokugo*. This was indeed a challenge as the text was mostly in uncommon kanji characters. On exam day we were given a blank sheet of paper and instructed to write the entire *Chokugo*. My memory was good in those days (maybe I did pick up some of Papa's talents) and I miraculously remembered every single kanji. The teacher graded the test paper then asked us to have our parents sign it and bring it back. Obviously Papa was pleased but said nothing and happily signed his name.

In addition to language, I studied Japanese classical dancing (*Sanbaso, Fuji Musume, Echigojishi, Harusame, Matsunomidori,* etc.) which also includes dressing in kimono, pigeon-toed walking, and proper manners. One of my dance teachers was a white Russian lady who earned her teaching credentials in Japan. Mrs. Brown was an excellent teacher, albeit a stern disciplinarian, and spoke fluent Japanese. (It seems that in the 1920s colonies of white Russians fled from the Russian Revolution into China, Japan and to America. Some of the white Russian communities still exist in Japan today).

I also learned the traditional Japanese tea ceremony with its ancient ritual of serving powdered green tea promising enlightenment, mental composure, elegant manners and etiquette. I also took lessons in ikebana the Japanese art of flower arrangement. Ikebana has many schools; I studied in the Sogetsu School for many years and earned several teaching certificates. Japanese calligraphy was taught to me by Buddhist priests in Oakland. Years later I picked it up again in Crystal City, TX and studied advanced calligraphy. Each of the aforementioned culture studies taught me concentration, patience and tranquility.

One Christmas, Papa bought Mama a mangle, a contraption used to press wrinkles out of damp laundry by pressing it between two horizontal rollers. Her reaction to this typical husband "Boy, won't my wife love what I got her!" gift was understandably mixed. He thought she could sit down and rest while the machine did the work. Actually it worked wonderfully on flats items like sheets but took a lot of time and skill to do men's shirts. Can you imagine during the Depression, we slept between ironed sheets? A luxury today!

Though none of us had any acting ambition, my siblings and I once put on a family play. We gave our parents front row seats and performed the skit entirely in Japanese. We portrayed our own family complete with parental spats; he was too hard on the children and she was too soft. Fortunately, Mama and Papa took the imitations like good sports. They laughed at the right places, clapped delightedly at our impersonations and, at the end, praised us for a good show. One unexpected though interesting outcome - they never argued in front of us again.

Ito Family at Russian River, 1930

Thanks to Papa's Model T, we took family trips to enjoy the beauty and diversity of California. During the summer we drove up the coast from Oakland and camped on the pebbly shores of the Russian River, about 75 miles north. Though primitive compared to today's cars, our Ford was a workhorse. We packed it to the gills with food, cooking equipment, tents, bedding, clothes plus two adults and four children. We were an Asian version of Steinbeck's Joad family migrating west.

In 1939 when I was 13, San Francisco hosted the World's Fair, Golden Gate International Exposition. A man-made island, Treasure Island, was created in San Francisco Bay between San Francisco and Oakland to be the site of the Fair. The exposition was to commemorate the completion of two bridges which were to forever change the Bay Area -- the San Francisco-Oakland Bay Bridge (dedicated 1936) and the

Golden Gate Bridge (dedicated 1937.) In those days, world's fairs were spectacular events and this was no exception. I was especially fascinated with the Japanese Pavilion with its demonstrations of silk weaving, classical doll-making, pearl diving and traditional elements. "Gayway" was a 40-acre "fun zone" featuring exotic foods, coasters, rocket ship and other thrill rides. This is where I tasted Coca-Cola for the very first time. I could only tolerate a few sips – this sweet and fizzy liquid burned my throat. It was a mystery to me why it was such a popular drink.

The Science Pavilion was especially interesting with its vast array of modern inventions and a peek into tomorrow. It predicted that someday we would watch movies and live shows in our own homes through a screened box called television; we would see the person on the other end of the telephone; highways would be multi-laned with clover-leafed exits; trains would run on monorails and much more. Today, some 70 years later, all these predictions have come true.

Baseball was hugely popular then and we kids were great fans of the Oakland Oaks of the Pacific League. Mama took us (four children) to see the games at Emeryville, a multi-transfer bus ride. It took a lot of courage and compassion for her to do this for us which I fondly recall with nostalgia and gratitude.

Our first family tragedy took place on November 3, 1939 when my sister Masa, aged 12, was killed in an automobile accident. She was run over and dragged by a car that had faulty brakes. At the hospital, in great pain and discomfort, Masa pleaded with Mama for *mizu*, *mizu*, *mizu* (water). The doctor advised against this request explaining she would die instantly if given water but she succumbed anyway. Mama never forgot that tragic scene and always regretted her decision. "If only I could have given her last taste of water, she would have died happily." Death is so final and it was painful to lose a sister who was not only my confidant but shared in all my activities. Along with beauty she had brains and though still 12 she had many admirers.

Religion was and still is loosely observed in most Japanese families, and, for us, was a comforting mix of Buddhist and Christian symbols, events and services. We had a small Buddhist altar where pictures of deceased relatives were honored. On Sundays, we children attended the local Japanese Methodist Church and learned of Jesus Christ and the Ten Commandments. Funerals were held at the local Buddhist temple (Buddhists are taught that upon death one becomes a Buddha, a very self-assuring belief.) Every summer, dressed in our *yukata* (cotton kimono) we participated in the Obon Festival held at the Buddhist Church. We never thought that Buddhism and the Christian Church were at odds. In fact, they seemed to teach a unified spiritual theme. People reincarnated into Buddha much like Christians went to heaven. It was simple and easy.

In 1940 the city of Oakland decided to build a modern roadway, the Nimitz Highway, through our neighborhood. 73 Sixth Street had been our home for 15 years but, in the name of progress, we moved. We settled in East Oakland into a two-story Victorian home near Foothill Boulevard. While we were looking for our new home, I experienced my first racial prejudice. Papa and I rang the doorbell of a "For Sale" house. The owner looked at us suspiciously, muttered, "it's already sold," and closed the door. Weeks later the For Sale sign was still up. It was a shock to realize that someone thought we were bad simply because we were Japanese. We eventually found a new house but I never forgot what prejudice felt like. But, it was to get a lot worse.

In our new home, we each had our own rooms. Though the house had a quaint Victorian exterior, the interior was quite modern with a lavender tiled bathroom. There was a large backyard with a chicken coop so we enjoyed fresh eggs daily plus a good size vegetable garden patch where we grew a lot of Swiss chard.

Now that we were all in school, Mama decided to go to work as a domestic to buy some new furniture for the new house. She was well liked by her employers and sometimes was hired on weekends. I often tagged along as her helper and travel companion.

In looking back on my childhood, my priorities were my studies then caring for my siblings' needs, bathing, cooking, housecleaning, sewing, mending, etc. It seems like I was always busy. Papa put up a sign which read "Time Is Money, Do Not Waste" and, like many of Papa's other teachings, it stuck with me.

Ancestral reverence is a strong trait in Japanese culture. Mama sent her precious savings to Japan for an expensive Hirawaki family tombstone which would elevate the family's social standing. Her siblings were elated and Mama was delighted to have restored pride back to the family.

Papa was also in a position to help his younger brother, Susumu, in Japan who had fallen ill with tuberculosis. Thanks to Papa, Uncle Susumu recuperated at a sanatorium on Oshima Island off the southern coast of Honshu for two years. Years later when we went to Japan, grateful Uncle Susumu thanked Papa for all his kindness. Susumu enjoyed longevity and lived to 103.

In the early 1940s, in our new all-white neighborhood, I attended Roosevelt High School for my sophomore year. Everyone was friendly but I found that academically Roosevelt did not prepare me for the University of California, my choice for college. In school I did not excel in any particular subject but I studied all my courses conscientiously and was able to maintain an A average. Fortunately, I was accepted by the highly-accredited Alameda High School for my junior year and attended for a few months before war broke out between the United States and Japan. Little did I realize that ensuing events were to change the course of my life.

Chapter II

Internment (1942-1945)

World War II started with Hitler's invasion of Poland on September 1, 1939. Eventually the world's most powerful nations fell into two sides with the formation of the Allies (United States, Great Britain, France, Russia) and the Axis (Germany, Italy, Japan). In the early 1940's, there was great speculation that Japan and U.S. might go to war but Papa was sure that war was unlikely due to the distance of the two countries separated by the vastness of the Pacific Ocean. Then the unbelievable happened. Japan bombed Pearl Harbor.

I was 16 and a junior at Alameda High School when war broke out. December 7th was a Sunday. and I was doing my homework with the radio turned on light music. Suddenly the announcer interrupted with the shocking news that Pearl Harbor was bombed by the Japanese. I was petrified and told Papa that I was too scared to go to school the next day. Why was I scared? We had recently moved to an all-white neighborhood and I felt self-conscious that I might be a victim of harassment because of my Japanese background. Papa assured me that this was a conflict between the two governments and that I should maintain a normal life. I am sure Papa was deeply concerned but he wanted me to stay calm and ride out the storm.

The following day, December 8th, Monday, I timidly rode the public bus to Alameda High School. The principal called an emergency school assembly and spoke of the crisis and reminded the students that there were loyal Japanese Americans among the student body and that they were to be treated with respect. As tense and scared as I felt, I did my best to act normal. My teachers were kind and sympathetic as were close non-Asian friends but it was not easy to stay calm amidst blaring anti-Japanese newspaper headlines and radio news.

The next day, President Roosevelt declared war on Japan. I lived a precarious existence then. Though my citizenship was American my ethnic heritage was Japanese. I knew no other country but the United States yet strangers looked upon me suspiciously as an enemy.

Shortly after December 7th, the FBI began an intense search for possible Japanese spies. Chief among their suspects were Isseis (first generation Japanese immigrants) who spoke only Japanese and lived in close-knit ethnic communities. My father, being bilingual, was appointed the official Alameda County Court House interpreter for the non-English speaking Japanese. He also held key posts in the Japanese community and was a prime target for investigation. The FBI interrogated Papa many times both at home and at the local FBI office but he was always released.

Those visits would start with a simple but chilling heavy knock on the front door in spite of the doorbell. Two dark suited men would flash their badges identifying themselves as FBI agents and barge into our home. They would go through everything in Papa's office, flinging papers into the air. Finding nothing they would abruptly depart leaving my sister and me to tidy up Papa's ransacked office.

In those days, Mr. J. Edgar Hoover, FBI Chief, and his staff were so powerful that to criticize or say anything negative about them labeled you as a "communist." So no matter how I felt "mum" was the word and it was decades later that I could reveal the truth.

On February 19, 1942, President Franklin Delano Roosevelt signed Executive Order 9066 which superseded the Constitution and the Bill of Rights leading to the forced internment of all Japanese living on the West Coast including citizens born in the United States. We, as well as, all our Japanese friends and neighbors, were among the 120,000 people arrested and interned in barbed-wire camps located in sparsely-populated areas of America's southwest.

Our only crime was our heritage.

I was in disbelief that the President of the United States had the power to overrule the Constitution and the Bill of Rights. However it was wartime and such things were possible. (Every year Feb.19th is recognized as the Day of Remembrance and Japanese American communities throughout the States hold ceremonies recalling the infamous event when 70 years ago Pres. Roosevelt signed Executive Order 9066 forcing 120,000 Japanese Americans into illegal detention camps.)

During those tense days, large posters were nailed to telephone posts much like posters in cowboy movies alerting citizens of bandits on the loose but in this case we were the bandits. The posters addressed to All Persons of Japanese Ancestry came in series. The first poster alerted all that curfew was in effect. Japanese were not allowed to be outdoors after dark. Luckily, my family was not inconvenienced by the curfew as after supper we did our homework and Papa visited his insurance clientele during the day. But the curfew seriously affected shop keepers, restaurateurs and those who had to commute after dark Poster #2 ordered all cameras, radios and weapons to be surrendered to the nearest police station. The curfew announcement was followed soon by a second set of posters ordering us to surrender cameras, short wave radios and weapons. None of us owned weapons but some families possessed valuable heirloom samurai swords that were handed down through generations. We had no prized samurai swords but recall surrendering a short wave radio and a Brownie box camera. We received receipts for whatever we turned in. The sword owners were assured that their valuables would be returned safely but alas things got misplaced and they lost their heirlooms. Poster #3 gave evacuation procedure informing us that we would be relocated out of the area to an unknown destination. We could take only what we could carry and $60 per family.

Rumors ran high about our being sent to the desert full of snakes and scorpions. It was difficult to pack as we knew very little of where we were going and for how long -- to a cold place or a hot place??? We ended up taking sleeping bags, sheets, blankets, knee high boots and I made sure to take my Webster's collegiate dictionary.

Papa sold the family car for a few hundred dollars. He set aside $60 for the trip and the balance he deposited in his bank account. Hawkers, human vultures who preyed on people's desperation and offered to buy their valuables for pennies, were everywhere and very much aware of the predicament we were in. Families with businesses, properties and homes had to either leave their belongings with friends, sell real cheap, or give them away or just abandon them.

Not knowing what lay ahead in this emergency situation, my parents thought that we should take a

family picture before any separation took place so we gathered for a family portrait. True to instinct, Papa was arrested by the government as a "potentially dangerous enemy alien" and separated from us for approximately two years.

The financial loss of homes, businesses and properties incurred by the Japanese due to their sudden evacuation is calculated in today's figures to be $10 billion.

Fortunately for us, we made arrangements with a Mexican friend, Juan Ortega and his wife, who moved into our house rent free. They did an excellent job of caring for our house during our long absence. Papa had a wonderful lawyer/friend, Mr. C.C. Culp, (whose grandson Robert was an actor). Years later I dealt with Mr. Culp representing my father, who was living in Japan, and finalized our finances. Not all were as fortunate as us.

Questions have arisen as to why only the Japanese, not the Germans or the Italians, were imprisoned. During World War II, Japan was part of the Axis countries. Why weren't the Germans and Italians also imprisoned? There are many unanswered questions. One of the reasons could be that in 1884 the United States government wanted menial Japanese laborers but Japan banned emigrants. However, strong pressure by the U.S. government emanating from the president relaxed this restriction. All went well as long as these Japanese were hard working, obedient and docile. As soon as they showed signs of initiative they were perceived as threats. The anti-Japanese campaign began with acts of violence, mob assaults, arson and expulsion. Soon these prejudices were institutionalized into law. The Japanese were denied citizenship, prohibited from holding important jobs, prohibited from marrying whites, denied rights to own or lease land and their children were prohibited from attending public schools.

Until 1941, the Japanese were mainly in farming and revolutionized agriculture when they installed irrigation in the California desert. The success of the Japanese farmers brought much rivalry and political unrest from the non-Japanese farmers. Many believe this had a strong contributing factor in the removal of the Japanese from the West Coast.

Another popular reason for the Japanese only incarceration was that Germans and Italians had intermarried, which meant that they had blended into the general population. However in the case of the Japanese, even if you were one-sixteenth Japanese you were imprisoned. Because to the Westerners all Asians look alike, our Chinese friends wore badges that read "I am Chinese" so as not to be mistaken for a Japanese.

Abiding by the instructions of the third poster, we were to assemble at the Oakland community center. I was deeply touched by the neighborhood grocery owner who came to bid us farewell and gave us a bag-full of sweets. His kindness brought tears to my eyes. At the gathering center I noted a few familiar Japanese faces and knew that we were at the right place -- a strange reassurance in this mysterious journey leading to where?

Our first introduction to camp life was to the Tanforan Race Track in south San Francisco to a horse stable which had been hurriedly swept and spray painted over cobwebs and dust. The place still smelled of hay and horse manure. We were a family of five people occupying the stable of one racehorse. A friend, whose family was also assigned to a stable, saw her parents weeping. She was five at the time and asked her older sister "Who died?"

The stalls had metal cots but no mattress. We were given large canvas bags and directed to a nearby haystack where we were to fill the bags with hay for bedding. The next day one of our new neighbors complained of a restless night and discovered a snake in his mattress. Some people thought they caught cold and stayed in bed only to get worse. They were later diagnosed as being allergic to hay and were given cotton mattresses.

In Tanforan we had roll calls twice a day. Our dignity was further discredited as our identity was no longer our family name but a six digit number. Meals were served at the grandstand so with eating utensils in hand we lined up in long queues for all our meals. Luckily, we brought our own aluminum mess kits as no utensils were provided. Time was plentiful so we didn't mind the long waiting line; besides we met a lot of friends. Food was ladled from large vats and served Army style onto waiting trays. Those who had gourmet taste went hungry.

School classes were set up haphazardly. There were no textbooks so we learned from lectures. We met by grades in different sections of the grandstand which also housed people who could not squeeze into the overcrowded stables. On Saturday nights the grandstand was used for make-shift talent shows.

A few days after we arrived in Tanforan, the FBI again came and this time arrested by father as "a potentially dangerous enemy alien." I witnessed my father being taken away and was in tears. A family friend approached me and said "Be brave, your father is an important person to us. You must behave with dignity worthy of his status." Papa wrote to us from Bismarck, North Dakota informing us that he was detained in a city jail for a few days but that he was healthy and well. Bismarck is one of the Justice Dept. camps where many Issei Japanese leaders were imprisoned. It is notable that in spite of the numerous arrests, no Japanese was ever been convicted of any war related crime against the United States.

After five months of stable living, we were transported by cattle cars to an unknown destination. Rumor had it that it would be one of the ten internment camps. We were moved like cattle into shade drawn trains going west for three days. We sat on hard wooden seats and every time we came to a station stop armed military police would walk the aisle to make sure we were behaving. Blinds were down but a few of us peeked to try to read the station name so that we could guess where we were headed.

Our train destination turned out to be Delta, Utah where a bus met us and drove us to what would

be our new home for the next three years - Topaz Internment Camp. All the buildings were Army barracks. A block consisted of two vertical rows of six buildings separated in the middle horizontally with two larger buildings which housed the mess hall and the laundry/latrine, shower facilities. We were assigned rooms according to family size.

Our assigned quarter was bare excepting for an iron potbelly stove, four metal cots and a single light bulb hanging from the ceiling. Each barrack consisted of six apartments of various sizes. Each family unit was separated from the adjoining room by sheet rock partitions not all the way up but part way. With the exposed top half - for "ventilating purpose" - one could hear conversations, couples' quarrels and heavy snoring at night. As it turned out, the lack of privacy didn't keep us from our rest; we kept active during the day so these strange noises became familiar sounds which lullabyed us to slumberland.

Our make shift community was called a "camp" but several different preceding adjectives arose: detention camps, internment camps, concentration camps, incarceration camps, relocation camps, etc. The government used the softer term "internment camps." These ten War Relocation camps were scattered in Arizona, Arkansas, California, Idaho, Utah and Wyoming. There were additional Justice Dept. camps, which held suspected criminals like Papa in New Mexico, North Dakota and Texas.

Today when I meet a fellow Japanese-American for the first time the usual greeting is "Hi! Which camp were you in?" We share common experiences as all the camps were built identical, same climate and all in remote godforsaken no man's land. Each camp was surrounded by barbed wire fences with armed sentries posted on all four corners. We had an incident in Topaz where an elderly man was arrowhead hunting in the desert and went beyond the boundary. The guard claims he yelled at the man to stop and when he didn't, he shot him in the back. The old man was deaf.

Each camp was self-governing. Each block elected a Block Manager, who served the needs of his block and was their representative at the Topaz administrative meetings. In addition there was the internee staffed camp hospital, an accredited elementary and high school, Buddhist, Catholic and Protestant churches and the general merchandise Co-op store. Camp wages were $8 a month for non-professionals and $16 a month for professionals so doctors and teachers drew the same salary.

Topaz Internment Camp is situated in central Utah's Sevier Desert near Delta City. Records reveal that Topaz was one of the places Brigham Young's scouts investigated as a possible home for the Mormons but was rejected as being unlivable. The elevation here is 5,000 feet above sea level. The beauty of high elevation is that on a cold clear winter night the heavenly stars shine like diamonds and appear almost touchable.

Summers were intensely hot (106 F) with frequent sandstorms. These dust storms would occur suddenly with no forewarning. We would run for cover from the fierce blinding wind that stung our faces and the ubiquitous rolling, thorny tumbleweeds. After each storm we had to sweep out the fine, talc like sand that seeped through the many cracks in the wall and floors of our quarter. We were always on the lookout for the deadly scorpions.

As hot as it was in the summer, the pendulum swung to the other extreme for the cold months. Winters were frigid cold (-30 F). In the morning our eyelashes were frozen and stuck together. Our source of heat was the coal fed iron pot belly stove in the room. Many a time when the coal pile located near the mess hall was depleted we tried to keep warm with government issued blankets to protect us from the bitter cold.

For the harsh winter, the Army supplied us with black Mackinaw jackets similar to the Navy pea coats. It was a one-size fits all and for a soldier it covered his hip but to us shorties, it was down to our ankles. So trudging to school during the frequent blizzards wearing our black Mackinaws, from the back, we must

have looked like a flock of South Pole penguins.

One amazing thing I remember was that although we were all Californians, seeing snow and experiencing Arctic cold for the first time in Topaz, very few caught cold. Snow days did not exist then, so we braved the blizzards from dawn to dusk. This was also pre-pants days for girls, so our legs and knees were exposed to the cold. But with all the walking (there were no cars or buses) we must have built up strong resistance to the cold.

My mother worked in the mess hall as did other parents. One of the dishes I recall was a frequent menu item -- tripe (cow's stomach). One month we counted 20 some odd servings. We ate tripe with teriyaki sauce, tripe with curry sauce, tripe smothered in ketchup, tripe covered with *shoyu* (soy sauce) but no matter how it was disguised it always tasted tripe. With Papa detained in another camp, Mama took over as our disciplinarian. We always sat together as family for dinner. Unfortunately, in many cases the father image as breadwinner was non-existent so the young ones, especially rowdy teenagers, did as they pleased showing a culturally shocking lack of respect to their parents.

Another jolting experience during imprisonment was the lack of privacy regarding hygiene, latrines and showers had no partition. I was a teenager then and at the height of modesty. I would go late at night to use the facility only to find that others had the same idea. One ingenious lady covered her head with a large paper bag. After months of complaining to the Block Manager, who in turn complained to the Camp Project Director, sheets were hung. Much later, wooden panel partitions were built. Toilet stall doors so basic a feature that we take them for granted became something we remembered in pre-camp life.

Papa and I corresponded by air letter regularly. He wrote very little about his life as his letters were closely scrutinized. Censoring was done by snipping. Once his letter came in a plain white envelope. The content was so cut up that it looked like a Christmas tree hanging. His letters encouraged us to keep busy constructively hinting to his favorite motto of 'Time is Money – Don't Waste.' After my high school graduation he advised me to continue at Topaz High and take all the postgraduate subjects offered and attend night school to study advanced Japanese. His letters always ended with: 'Be Strong in Mind, Body and Spirit.'

Years later I always included this phrase when I spoke to young students about my internment experience. "Life is full of ups and downs. As you young students wean away from your parents' protection, learn to be a strong individual. Expand your knowledge to strengthen your Mind; consume healthy food and exercise your Body; enhance your Spirit with an optimistic view on life." This mindset has helped me through life and I have passed it on to my three sons.

In this communal living everyone had a job. Mine was to attend school. Coming from an Asian immigrant family, education was all important. I remember those Oakland days, though Japanese lived in scattered neighborhoods throughout the city, all my Nisei friends made honor rolls in their respective schools. This is not to say that we were any smarter but we applied ourselves. Our parents typically said very little about how important good grades were but we knew what was expected of us. It was our cultural upbringing that in all our behavior we were not to bring "haji" or shame to our people.

Camp school thus became a congregation of achievers. We had a class of honor roll students vying for top grades. I recall our Caucasian English teacher lamenting "I can't grade on curves. They are all "A" students." Competition was keen and I never studied so hard. This turned out to be a blessing as I was totally immersed in schoolwork with no time to grieve over the injustice surrounding me. In later years, one of the Caucasian teachers recalled with sadness that every morning when we pledged our allegiance to the American flag, she always got a lump in her throat when, with our right hands over our hearts, we recited '… with liberty and justice for all.'

School was bare-bones with no library or chemistry labs. School subjects were the standard: English, Higher Math, Chemistry, Physics, etc. Our extra curriculum activities consisted of the chorus, science, language, thespian, future farmers, etc. There were also numerous sport activities, i.e. track, basketball, football, and baseball. Athletes participated in intramural competition with the neighboring town Delta. I was voted to head a Home Economics group where we discussed interior decorating, simple cooking and ideas to enhance our dull barrack rooms.

In spite of the barren desert, Topaz High School's first graduation was comparable to any in the states. I was one of the 210 graduating seniors and enjoyed all the festivities including attending the senior prom and wearing the traditional cap and gown. From the "outside" - a terminology we used quite often referring to the outside world or outside of camp, we were able to order our beautiful blue yearbook with snapshots of all the graduating seniors plus our rented, smart looking navy caps and gowns. We autographed each other's '43 Ramblings yearbooks with positive and optimistic comments. Despite our imprisonment we were elated to have climbed the first rung in "Life's Ladder to Adulthood.'

One of my poignant memories was when an 18 year old youth received his Army draft notice. Should he refuse the draft, stay in camp and care for his elderly parents or should he enlist like a loyal American? Many felt that this was the crucial time to prove loyalty to America in spite of adversities. I knew of one family where the son was obedient to his parents but also wanted to enlist. His father was adamantly against his son's intent to volunteer. Just hearing about it wrenched my heart.

Coming home from school one day, I noticed a gold star flag displayed on a barrack window. It brought a lump in my throat as I had heard that an elderly couple lived there and the gold star flag indicated a son had given his life for his country. How ironic that the son gave his life for his country while his elderly parents were obeying the law of the same land living behind barbed wire.

On January 28, 1943, Secretary of War Henry Stimson announced the formation of a special all-Nisei 5,000-man combat unit known as the 442nd Regimental Combat Team. Army recruiters were sent to visit the ten camps. Those who registered were required to answer loyalty questionnaires.

The War Relocation Authority failed to prepare camp residents by educating them about the registration. The reaction reached its greatest intensity at the Tule Lake Internment Camp. Poor preparation by the camp administration combined with deception, force, fines, arrests and threats of long prison terms led to massive resistance to the questionnaire.

The document, designed by the War Relocation Authority to test the loyalty of alien and citizen Japanese Americans living in the camps, read:

- Question 27 -- Are you willing to serve in the armed forces of the United States on combat duty, wherever ordered?

- Question 28 --Will you swear unqualified allegiance to the United

States from any and all attack by foreign or domestic forces, and foreswear any form of allegiance to the Japanese Emperor, or any other foreign government, power, or organization?

Positive answers to 27 and 28 made the youths eligible for service in the Army. The recruitment was a moderate success as over 3000 volunteered from the ten camps. Those who gave "no" answers as a means to protest the mass removal and detention, referred to as the "No-No Boys" were stigmatized as being "disloyal trouble makers" and were removed to the Tule Lake (CA) Segregation Center so as not to corrupt the "loyal" internees.

I stood on the sidelines and witnessed both sides with empathy. It was indeed a most difficult time not knowing which fork in the road to take. It was one of the few times when my parents were glad I was born a female.

Emotions grew heated during the "loyalty questioning" but nonetheless the government sent recruitment teams to all the camps seeking Army volunteers for the 442nd and the 100th battalion to fight in Europe. Those knowledgeable in the Japanese language were recruited for the Military Intelligence Service and sent to the Pacific.

Some 70 years later in November 2011, the soldiers of the aforementioned units were honored in Washington DC with the Congressional Gold Medals.

In attendance were the elderly veterans and close relatives of deceased soldiers who travelled from even distant Hawaii.

Most of the internees endured the camp experience for three years. It was possible to leave camp for schooling or employment provided resettlement was to the East. Returning to West Coast was disallowed. The majority of my peers are reluctant to speak about internment; like a rape victim, innocent but embarrassed and uncomfortable to talk about it.

Finally, after three years of internment, the government allowed the internees to return to their homes on the West Coast. They were given a meager travel allowance of $25. Many faced prejudice as the public still had strong animosity towards the Japanese, especially those who lost loved ones in the Pacific. Many stayed at local churches, lived in small trailer courts or moved East where people were more hospitable.

Prior to the closing of Topaz, Papa was allowed to come to Topaz to help us pack for our next move -- Crystal City Family Internment Camp. We had not seen Papa since our stay in Tanforan. Then, his hair was mostly black with a few strands of white. After a few years away from the family, his hair had turned snow white. Asians do not show their emotions, but it was apparent that the separation hit Papa severely as he worried about the well-being of our family. The mystery of why my father was not released like other fathers came to light when a family friend confided in me. "Your father is a strong and just man, and was not manipulated by interrogators. He did not squeal on others seeking merits for his own release. He is a hero to many of us." Papa was educated, knew the Law and was mature enough to see through the questioners' tactics.

From Topaz Relocation Camp which was run by the War Relocation Authority, we were transferred to the Crystal City Family Internment Camp, the only family internment camp operated by the Justice Department where detainees held the status of "prisoners of war." The only way for the family to be together was in this family camp in Texas. It was situated southwest of San Antonio 40 miles from the U.S.-Mexican border. In addition to the Japanese, there were Germans, Italians and Japanese from Bolivia and Peru.

We were assigned to "victory huts" no larger than 15' x 15' made of plywood with no insulation. In the summer, it was like living in an oven and in the winter it was drafty and cold. During a bad storm, the wind would blow out windows, doors and roofs. The roof had metal sheeting and the frequent downpour raised the noise level equal to a dozen elves pounding the roof with sledge hammers. Food was much better than Topaz as we bought our own food at the local commissary and cooked it in our small kitchenette over kerosene stoves.

In spite of the Crystal City's international population, the Japanese had their own social community. The language school was patterned a la Japan and we studied the school curriculum -- math, algebra, geometry, history, calligraphy, grammar, composition, literature and science from Japanese  textbooks. I had difficulty reading and understanding the texts but in due time was able to keep up with my classmates. Our teachers were mostly Buddhist priests from Hawaii. I understand in Peru and Bolivia the students attend Japanese schools rather than the native schools, so these students spoke fluent Japanese and excelled in our classes.

Outside of school, I joined the Girl Scout troop organized by a lady physician, Dr. Mori of Hawaii. I welcomed marching outdoors after being indoors most of the day doing my homework.

While we were living in Texas, we heard and read about the triumphant U.S. bombings in the Pacific war. Japan was losing badly but the staunch Issei Japanese were swayed by the shortwave radio news from Brazil that Japan was in fact winning the Pacific battles. We were getting conflicting battle news but. of course, the Isseis sided with their homeland. August 14, 1945 V-J Day was heralded by sirens and whistles. Unlike the scene at New York's Times Square, I don't recall any outward signs of jubilation in our Texas Prisoner of War camp but everyone was elated that war was over.

Papa had lived in the States for 38 continuous years and the last five years had not been easy. He never mentioned it outright but the toll of being separated from his family and put into harsh detention prisons like the California jail, remote camps in Santa Fe, New Mexico and Bismarck, North Dakota were unpleasant events in America. He yearned to see his siblings in northern Japan and to live out his years there. When he learned that he and his family were eligible for free passage to Japan he immediately signed up as did many of his peers in Crystal City. The elite group of "prisoners of war" (mostly diplomats) returned to Japan on the luxury ship **Gripsolm,** however the Crystal City prisoners of war were to return to Japan on the **S.S. Matsonia**. Papa was optimistic that he might even be able to teach English on a college level.

I was offered several college scholarships and was tempted to stay behind in the States while the family went to Japan. I gave this fork-in-the-road decision much thought but being the eldest child of aging parents I felt a strong obligation to stay with the family. I have never regretted this decision.

We lived in Crystal City almost a year, arriving in January and departed in early December of 1945. We packed our belongings, rode the train west to Seattle then boarded the **S.S. Matsonia** bound for Japan arriving there on Christmas Day in 1945.

Chapter III

Japan
(1945-1950)

Our voyage to Japan was the result of a very difficult decision that Papa made for the family. He had been in the States for thirty-eight continuous years but kept in touch with his siblings by letters. When offered a free passage to Japan (presumably covered by the U.S. government) many thoughts must have preyed on his mind. How would his children adjust in Japan? To them Japan would be a strange and defeated country. If he returned to Oakland, California right after a war with Japan, would anyone hire a sixty year-old Japanese national? Weighing the matters of survival and pride, he ultimately decided that the family should move to Japan. Other families we knew also decided to relocate to Japan which meant we wouldn't be going alone. Papa was optimistic that his fluency in English and Japanese would help get him employment in Japan. And, he reasoned, his children's studies in Japanese language and culture would ease their transition to this, for them, foreign land that they would be seeing for the first time. Mama was supportive of Papa as she too had siblings in Tokyo and had lost contact with them during the war years. So Papa, with his stoic "now or never" attitude, decided that Japan was where we should go. And that, was that.

We were once again a family of five (Papa, Mama, Yone, Shigeru and me). That was reassuring but nothing else in our lives was and so I felt lost and tremendously confused. I'm sure Yone (then 16) and Shigeru (then 13) had similar thoughts. But we were obedient children and did what our parents asked. This was especially true for me, the oldest child whose primary responsibility was to safeguard our parents.

We packed our meager belongings from Crystal City and boarded a westward-bound train for Seattle, Washington. From the port of Seattle we embarked in early December 1945 on the **S.S. Matsonia** bound for Japan. Our bunk mates were the Utsushigawa family whose relatives lived in northern Japan – same as Papa. Mr. U sported an unusually handsome beard and I enjoyed watching him comb it every morning as part of his grooming routine. He was accompanied by his amiable wife and bright and energetic daughter, Sumi, who was my sister Yone's age. Since Mr. U and Papa both originated from northern Japan, it was decided that the two families would travel together back to the northern Tohoku region. The U family was looking forward to a reunion with their two older daughters who had been stranded in Japan during the war.

Our passage took 17 days and was made pleasant by the companionship of friends from Crystal City, who like Papa felt that Japan offered a better life. December is a rough sailing month but I recall a fairly calm voyage and few seasick passengers.

The **Matsonia** anchored in Uraga Bay (Tokyo Bay) on a cold December 25, 1945, four months after VJ day. This was the same port that Commodore Matthew Perry landed some 50 years before opening diplomatic and commercial relations between Japan and the United States. At the port city of Uraga, we were greeted by a large American flag unmistakably proclaiming that the United States was now in charge. While in Crystal City, Papa had heard rumors via shortwave radio communique from Brazil that: "Japan had won the war and furthermore she would never surrender unconditionally." I saw tears in Papa's eyes as he gazed at the Stars and Stripes waving over Japan; he must have finally realized that any hope that Japan had not been defeated was, in an instant, utterly extinguished.

We disembarked from the **S.S. Matsonia** to the Uraga Receiving Center where refugees from America, Bali and Sumatra were processed. The evacuees from southeast Asia were still clad in their tropical clothing (women in light weight sarong and men in shorts). Although it was freezing, no warm clothing was provided for them, so many of them died of exposure. They literally froze to death. Their corpses were placed in pine coffins and stacked in a room whose glass shoji door we walked past every time we went to the dining room. The authorities told us that a truck would come to pick up the corpses when the count reached ten but that didn't happen while we were there. Due to the cold weather there was no unpleasant smell. But, this stack of coffins, nearly visible every time we ate, became a regular if grim aspect of our stay there. Those of us from America felt pity on these wretched evacuees from southeast Asia but that sympathy reflected much of our own unenviable lives.

The food at Uraga was simply unfit for human consumption and we longed for the American internment camp food which we had always disparaged. The miso soup contained unwashed green vegetables - dirt settled in the bottom of the bowl. In lieu of rice we were served grain husk, normally discarded during processing. It was quite obvious that we were undesirables and were treated as such. This was understandable as Japan was barely coping with the obliteration of their national pride, widespread destruction and a starving population during the winter months. Their hands were full just taking care of their own. The bitter reality was that we were undesirables in the States and undesirables in Japan.

We contacted our nearest kin upon our arrival in Japan by telegram and the Japanese government issued us free railway tickets to our destination. After bidding sayonara to our Crystal City friends in Uraga we (the Itos and the Utsushigawa families) started on our long trek north. We first took the local train to Ueno station where we would make a transfer.

Travelling north, I saw firsthand the aftermath of war-devastated Japan. Yokohama, Kawasaki, Tokyo -- once thriving cities – were now wastelands pocked by blackened skeletal ruins. The US military's firebomb campaign on Tokyo where structures were almost entirely made of wood and packed side-by-side was apocalyptically effective. Only a few standing brick walls, chimneys and scarred trees remained. Our faces pressed against the windows of our train, we witnessed

 an endless scene of homeless and starving men, women and children searching through debris for their homes and belongings. The land between Yokohama to Tokyo, two formerly bustling cities, was now one immense flat field of ruin and devastation.

At Ueno Station, where we changed trains, I saw many once proud Imperial soldiers, now crippled and homeless, begging for food. It seemed that nearly everyone was starving. Families ate grass like cows and stuffed putrid garbage into their mouths, when they could find it. It was a time of the "survival of the fittest" and *kaidashi* (black market shopping) was the way to exist. Men and women carried huge *furoshiki* (cotton sheets used for bundling and transporting goods) filled with silk kimonos, blankets, family heirlooms and sometimes furniture to sell or barter to farmers living in the north for their uncooked crops.

We rode the *kaidashi* train and every stop was a mad scramble of people getting off and on. When a door was blocked, they would break the windows to exit. The desperate mob screamed and shouted in the northern Tohoku dialect which sounded rough and menacing. I recalled Akira Kurosawa's classic black and white movie *Yojinbo* where unshaven, un-bathed, ill-clad ruffians acted more like animals than humans. But, this was no movie. It was a "life or death" situation for them and I was wide-eyed and terrified American 20 year old living in this nightmarish world.

Sitting next to us on the train was a young Japanese soldier who told us he was returning to Hakodate (Hokkaido). Hearing of our plight, he kindly dug into his bag and produced *onigiri* (rice balls) for us to share. It was made from top-grade white rice and tasted more delicious than anything I could imagine. We thanked him profusely. To this day, no *onigiri* has ever tasted so good.

Finally, we arrived at Papa's younger brother's home in Wakayanagi. It was a typical farmer's home with sparse furnishings. Farmhouses in the area were all two-story structures. During the winter when the frequent and heavy snow engulfed the first floor, occupants entered and exited their houses from an outside door on the second floor. The ceiling shelves held rows of cabbages, food for the winter months. My aunt didn't seem too happy to see us and I could understand why -- their family of eight had barely enough to eat. Now, they had to suddenly share their precious food with five more mouths. I felt guilty, but Papa assured me that this was temporary situation. Besides, he explained when Uncle Susumu was sick with TB and institutionalized for several years, Papa paid all the bills. Uncle's family consisted of three daughters and three sons, the youngest in kindergarten. Uncle was a devout Christian and did some volunteer church work but neither his wife nor children showed any religious interest.

Even more awkwardly, we had some difficulty understanding each other. We spoke standard Japanese and they understood us, however their Japanese was the Tohoku brogue. To us, they sounded gruff, primitive and unintelligible.

I recall one cold snowy day shortly after our arrival in Wakayanagi when we as a family sat around the *kotatsu* (charcoal heated stove) to seriously discuss our family's precarious present and gravely uncertain future. The reality was that we had no jobs (hence no income), no home of our own; and no plan for the future.

But from that meeting came action plans for each of us. Papa and I would find jobs. The only organization hiring was the occupying United States forces. Local economies and businesses were largely destroyed or barely surviving. One big problem was the nearest office was in Sendai, a good three-hour train ride away, or six hours of commuting. We travelled to Sendai, applied for jobs and were accepted. The irony of my being an American citizen, locked up for years by my own country, escaping to a country just defeated by America, then becoming employed by America was almost too ludicrous to imagine.

My younger siblings, Yone and Shigeru, would attend the local Japanese school. Attending school was no major problem as they both spoke Japanese fluently.

I feared prejudice for Yone and Shigeru but they reported that they encountered none. Surprisingly, the fact that we were from America actually conferred some measure of prestige. No kid wants to stick out so Shigeru asked Mama to sew patches on his clothes to make them look worn out and had his hair crew cut so he could look like his classmates. Yone's main complaint was that sitting Japanese-style on her knees all day made her legs go numb and straightening them out after many hours was painful.

Mama's job would be to stay home to cook, launder, sew and to tend to our needs.

Our language skills proved key in our new jobs in Sendai. Papa was assigned to work for the Legal Department as an interpreter/translator. One of his majors at college was law. I was assigned to the Public Health/Sanitation Department as secretary/interpreter. My job was to accompany the Public Health Officers on a number of trips to nearby hospitals to speak to local doctors and officials on the use of DDT and medications for sex-related diseases. With Papa's help and a good dictionary, I was able to translate and interpret these professional presentations.

Commuting was super-long and tiring but we felt fortunate to have jobs. Papa and I would rise each morning at four a.m., eat breakfast and leave the house by five. We would take the local tram, transfer to the government rail system to arrive at work by nine. We would reverse the routine and return home after dark, eat supper, bathe and sleep. This was our routine for many, many months.

One day we left for work at the usual five a.m. on a snowy day which later developed into a blizzard. We left work that day, made it back to Wakayanagi but found that the local tram had stopped running due to the hazardous conditions. We had no choice but to walk along the tram tracks if we were to get home that night. We began trudging through the snow. Then we experienced a frightening situation that I will never forget. The tram tracks continued on to a trestle over a steep gorge. How on earth were we able to get across? If we stopped walking we might have frozen to death so we got down on our hands and knees and crawled on all fours clinging desperately to the thin, cold rails in the fierce winds. Papa kept saying to me, "Don't look down, just look ahead!" It was indeed a harrowing experience! Several cold and wet hours later, we made it home utterly exhausted. After a welcome soak in the *ofuro* (Japanese hot bath), we went straight to bed knowing that the next day's commute was only a few hours away.

At the Sendai station I met a young lady who took the same train as I did. Himeko Togashi and I became friends and exchanged daily happenings. When I told her about my and Papa's six-hour daily commute she was shocked. With her parents' approval, Himeko generously offered to put Papa and me up in her large home. Her family was devoutly Catholic. They were caretakers and lived in the mansion-like parsonage. I was elated and accepted her kind invitation. Mama joined us to set up housekeeping in Sendai and my siblings followed after their school year ended. Our friendship endured through the years; Himeko even visited me after I moved to the States.

Things were going very nicely, but the city girl in me wanted to move on. Ever since we moved to Japan, I realized that I was more American than Japanese and had no desire to live in Japan permanently. However, as the eldest in the family I had responsibilities to fulfill before I could pursue my own goals. Priority one was to ensure my parents' comfort and well-being. I wanted buy them a house but I had no money. It was all a dream, a secret dream that I shared with no one. I felt that step one towards the fulfillment of that dream was to find a job in Tokyo. Eventually, I admitted my desire to move to the big city to my parents and they gave me their blessing.

Through a friend I found a family who was willing to rent me a spare room in Tokyo. I also found employment as a clerk-typist at the 720th Military Police Battalion at Hibiya Park across from the Imperial moat. Setsuko Kudo, a veteran worker there, took me under her wing and treated me with great kindness. (Setsuko is a California Nisei who married a young Japanese newspaper reporter and lived in London for many years. Her husband, Shinichiro Kudo, eventually became president of **Mainich Shinbun**, one of Japan's leading newspapers.). I have cherished my friendship with Setsuko for over 60 years and visited her in Tokyo whenever I was there.

My job at the 720th Military Battalion was that of a mere clerk-typist but to the top brass who wanted MP (Military Police) tickets "fixed" (destroyed) I had clout. The MPs that I worked with thought it strange that all the Japanese girls working there had American names like Susie, Mabel, Cherry, etc. whereas I, an American, had only a Japanese name – Kiyo. They decided "Jean" was a suitable name for me and so Jean I became. The name has stayed with me all these years. I liked my nickname as it automatically categorized me as an American.

I lunched everyday with my fellow workers at the Dai Ichi Building, General Headquarter for five-star General Douglas MacArthur, Supreme Commander of the U.S. Occupation Force with full command of Japan. Everyone, American and Japanese alike, were in awe of his authority and towering presence. My co-workers and I, along with his many admirers, witnessed his daily arrival and departure, each as grand a ceremony as if it were the Emperor himself.

In those days the work force classifications were: Military Personnel, Civil Service Workers, Foreign Nationals and Japanese Nationals. Despite being an American I was classified as a Foreign National until I was able to prove to the U.S. Consulate my American citizenship. Due to post-war turmoil, I did not have a US passport. Our passage on the **Matsonia** and entry into Japan did not require one. But, now, it made a huge difference. I made numerous discouraging and emotionally draining trips to the U.S. Consulate in Yokohama to get citizenship affidavits. But once I finally received papers proving my U.S. citizenship, I was relieved and overjoyed! Then and now, American citizenship is something millions of people in every country in the world yearn for. Many Americans take their citizenship for granted. But, when you lose it as I nearly did, you quickly realize how truly precious it is and how lucky we are.

One day, I was taken by complete surprise when I was asked to teach conversational English to a distinguished Japanese family in Yoyogi, the neighborhood where I lived. The elderly father was a retired cabinet minister whose position was equivalent to our Secretary of the Interior. My students included Minister and Mrs. Yuzawa and their four adult children. Our weekly lessons grew into friendship and soon I was treated like family. At one of their parties, I met Guen Inokuma, a renowned artist who studied under Henri Matisse in Paris. Mr. Inokuma wanted to paint me for the cover of **Shinjoen,** a popular ladies' magazine. At first I was hesitant, but Mrs. Yuzawa assured me that both the artist and the

magazine were honorable and I ended up posing for two cover issues.

My friendship with the Yuzawa family and ties with the painter Inokuma were exciting opportunities, but they were not the only ones. And, for all of these, I thank Mama. You see, my mother, by working for years for the Oyama diplomat family, learned the social graces, elevated language and refined manners that characterize Japanese upper class. She took great pains to pass them onto her children. We were never rich and often very poor. But, I learned to speak and act like those cultured and wealthy. And these skills opened many doors for me, as you shall see.

Rumors were circulating that private companies in Tokyo were paying wages in U.S. dollars as against the Japanese yen paid by most companies. That was a huge advantage as the yen was relatively frail. So, now newly armed with a U.S. passport, I decided to seek employment with an American company.

During my lunch hour I went to a nearby women's hotel, found a comfortable chair near a telephone and, using the directory, called American companies stationed in Tokyo to ask whether they had jobs and if they paid salaries in dollars. I started with letter "A". By the third day of calling, I had reached the letter "I" and reached the Tokyo branch of International Business Machines- I.B.M. The person who answered said yes, he was looking for a typist, a stenographer, an interpreter and a translator. Since I was able to do all four, I was hired on the spot and was offered a generous salary – in U.S. dollars. I worked hard and with alacrity. Fairly soon, I was promoted to office manager and was given a car with driver to handle my many diversified duties.

The Tokyo office maintained all IBM equipment (computers) in the Far East -- Japan, Guam and  Okinawa. IBM's primary customer was the U.S. military who used IBM mainframes to process their enormous payroll, track statistics and other enormous data processing chores. The magnitude of the information processing IBM did for the military was absolutely astronomical. They performed daily, weekly and monthly data processing for every soldier, civil service worker, spouse, etc. in the entire Far East. Ten IBM customer engineers were sent from the States on a rotational basis to service these big machines. In those days, working for IBM meant a strict dress code, adherence to ethical conduct and almost a cult-like allegiance to the company's philosophies and values.

Customer engineers never deviated from their uniform of dark business suits, white shirts, conservative ties and leather satchels in which they carried their tools. In reality they were well-dressed repairmen.

Part of my job was to contribute articles about happenings in Tokyo and all of Japan for the company's international newspaper, *Business Machines,* read by IBM

employees around the world. These articles covered such events as sailing, skiing, and parties galore for arriving and departing employees. We all worked hard but enjoyed the Tokyo life which I wrote about as engagingly as I could. I guess my descriptions of the exciting and exotic fun we were having found a receptive audience. Soon there was a waiting list of employees requesting assignment to the Tokyo office. Imagine people *wanting* to come to a country just defeated in a horrific war!

There is a Japanese expression *on gaeshi* (returning an obligation). For me, working for IBM was such an honor that I felt I had to return the favor. I decided that I would help support the company by purchasing IBM stock. In those days a single share cost a whopping $200 but I began by buying partial shares through the employee deduction program. My tiny but regular contributions allowed me to participate in IBM's historic rise with price increases, regular stock splits and reliable dividends that would last for decades. Watching my stock portfolio grow, I soon realized that my dream of buying that house for Mama and Papa just might come true! So I worked hard at my job, spent very little and saved, saved, saved. With help from my cousin Takashi Hasegawa, a senator in the Diet, the Japanese Parliament, I bought a modest stucco bungalow in Yokohama close to the main train station. Three years after arriving in Japan, we finally lived under one roof as a family -- Papa, Mama, Shigeru and me.

About this time, sister Yone became disenchanted with Japan and returned to the States settling in San Francisco. She found a kind Jewish family who took her in while she attended a nearby college. Brother Shigeru enrolled at St. Joseph's, a Catholic boys' school on the Bluff in Yokohama. Papa found work at the Yokohama Chamber of Commerce writing all the English texts for pamphlets and editing all the official correspondence. Mama took care of the house, made many friends in the neighborhood and enjoyed monthly trips to nearby Tokyo to see Kabuki shows.

As I commuted daily from Yokohama to Tokyo by rail, I witnessed the amazingly speedy rebuilding of postwar Japan, now considered one of the greatest economic and political achievements of the modern age. Shops and homes were built and functional in the blink of an eye. Japanese scaffolding in those days consisted of tall bamboos tied with hemp by workers in indigo blue *happi* coats and thick padded black *zoris* (heavy cloth shoes worn by laborers). I remember a fire had destroyed a small shop and a camera-happy IBM'er remarked, "I'm going to take a picture of that tomorrow." Someone else replied, "It'll probably be rebuilt by then." And, it probably was.

One day after an unusually long walk with the family dog, "Queenie", Papa came home quite impressed with the beautiful Foreigners Cemetery on the Yokohama Bluff with panoramic views of the city and harbor. Only non-Japanese could buy plots there. He said to me, "Kiyo, you're a foreigner. You could buy a plot there." So I did. At the time, my parents were still healthy but I envisioned the inevitable. On a clear day, Mt. Fuji is visible in the distance. With its premier location regally protected by tall black iron gates embellished in gold, it is one of the outstanding cemeteries in Japan. Mama died early at age 58 while Papa lived until age 93. I'm sure my parents are proud to be there. And I visit them every time I travel to Japan.

My life was challenging, interesting and enjoyable. I made many Japanese friends and enjoyed dating both Americans and Japanese, usually going to dinner and then a movie. But, deep in my heart, I longed to return to the States single and start my life afresh. One day I approached my boss at IBM. "Fritz, I am now ready to return to the States. Is it possible to continue working for IBM in the States?" He replied,

"Jeanie, you name the city and I will guarantee you an IBM job." Ever since I was a child I was in awe of New York City, so without hesitation I blurted out, "New York City!"

I had lived in Japan for five years and was now ready to return home. I could not have been more excited! I had fulfilled my personal master plan. My parents had a comfortable home and a family resting plot. A job at IBM was waiting for me in New York City, a place I had long dreamed of seeing. I splurged and bought myself a luxurious Japanese mink coat and prepared to move.

It was sad and difficult saying sayonara to my parents. Friends honored me with some incredible gifts - Mme. Yuzawa whom I taught English, surprised me with a gorgeous hand embroidered crepe silk kimono she had received from Empress of Japan. Papa handed me an envelope containing US $500 -- more than he could afford -- but I accepted it with gratitude. Later, I used all that money to buy IBM stock in Papa's name and they continued to steadily appreciate. That stock made Papa a shareholder for the first time in his life. He began studying the market daily and soon became an active investor.

On a beautiful, jubilant day in June, 1950, I boarded a ship back to America. So many emotions! Excitement, optimism, sadness, all whirling through my head! Many friends came to see me off at the Yokohama pier. I stood on the deck and clutched strands of brightly colored tape whose other ends were held by my waving, cheering friends on the pier. Two of those strands in my hand were literally my last physical connection with Mama and Papa for many years. As the ship began leaving, the tape grew taut then snapped and fluttered down to the water. I was 24 and now truly on my own for the first time in my life.

Chapter IV

New York City

Upon my arrival in San Francisco I taxied to the St. Francis Hotel in midtown and enjoyed the first few days as a tourist walking the avenues luxuriating in my brand new mink coat (ideal for Frisco's June days), riding the trolley, lunching at Fisherman Wharf and enjoying sushi at Japanese town. It was nostalgic to return to stateside atmosphere especially window shopping and reading all the signs in English. For the first time in half a decade, I finally felt at home surrounded by things American.

As happy as I was to be back in the States, I couldn't wait to get to New York City, my lifelong dream. To get there I took my first plane ride and kept my nose pressed against the window the entire trip. My former IBM Tokyo boss Fritz Armstrong, who had himself relocated to New York very recently, met me at LaGuardia airport – it was so wonderful to see a familiar face! As we taxied to Manhattan, Fritz pointed out sights that I'd long seen in magazines. We dined at a popular steak house while reminiscing about the "good old days in Tokyo." It was indeed a dazzling feeling to be in the capital of the world!

Fritz managed to get me a job at IBM's Watson Scientific Computing Laboratory at Columbia University. In fact, IBM gave me a choice - working at the Watson Lab. or at World Headquarters at 590 Madison Avenue. Perhaps due to Papa's scholarly bent, I chose the academic atmosphere in uptown Manhattan and became secretary to Dr. W. J. Eckert, a world-renowned astronomer and director of the Watson Laboratory. A frequent visitor was Dr. Robert Oppenheimer, nuclear physicist from Princeton. Another luminary in the world of physics, Dr. Llewelyn Thomas was a senior staff member. There were 60 or more PhDs. I was in awe of the caliber of scientists I would be supporting and couldn't imagine what the letter of recommendation contained. In addition my secretarial chores, I was office manager and head of the steno pool.

We used the latest IBM typewriters which used not cloth ribbons but ones made from extremely thin paper, the first time I'd seen such things. Typed pages looked as if they came from a print shop: very professional, but mercilessly unforgiving if you made a mistake. This was decades before computers and word processing made editing and correcting a routine and frequent aspect of typing. When your finger hit a key, the character instantly and permanently printed on the page. And, typos were an absolute no-no. By then I was highly seasoned typist and made very few errors but when I came to the last few lines of a page I slowed down and carefully henpecked the last sentence. The job was immensely challenging but equally rewarding.

After settling in my new job, I moved from the YWCA in downtown Manhattan to Columbia University's International House. It was summer-time and dorms were available. International House was closer to my work and I had the opportunity to meet many foreign students. In the fall I found a studio apartment a short walking distance to work.

The Watson Laboratory, located on the campus of Columbia University, was one of the preeminent scientific computing labs in the world and closely associated with the school, its elite faculty and brainy students. One of the Lab's projects was to break down the structure of proteins using the immense calculating power of IBM computers. Another was the development of an astronomical data book with the exact positions of planets in our solar system from 1400 to 2200. Years later, NASA depended on the accuracy of this data for their space exploration program. I also attended a few night courses at Columbia University studying early America literature.

I remember attending my first IBM shareholders' meeting held at the Waldorf Astoria Hotel. I had the opportunity to meet Mrs. Watson, the wife of the founder, and her family. Back then, shareholders' meetings were small, intimate affairs. We sat down to an elegant luncheon followed by a short business meeting. Today IBM stockholders meetings are held in huge auditoriums to accommodate the thousands of shareholders who attend.

On Sundays I attended the local Japanese Methodist Church and met a few Japanese-American newcomers to the Big Apple like myself. I soon learned to navigate NYC's public transportation system and happily played the tourist on weekends. Papa visited New York when he was young and gave me a list of "must-sees." High on the list was Cleopatra's Needle in Central Park, as well as, top museums and the zoo. I especially enjoyed riding the narrated cruise around Manhattan Island and the short ferry ride to Staten Island which cruised past the Statue of Liberty.

At the Lab, I met an attractive blond Czech girl who started working there about the same time I did. We became good friends. Kay commented that though we were both new arrivals my social life seemed much busier than hers. I suggested she attend the nearest Czech church which she did and her social life perked up. The camaraderie among the women staff at the Watson Lab was friendly and upbeat. Though we were from different ethnic and cultural backgrounds, we shared much in common as IBM'ers. We were also mostly new to the city. We worked hard during the day and never missed the latest show at Rockefeller Center, attended Broadway matinees, and ate at popular eateries.

I remember vividly one incident. A bunch of us girls went to a Broadway stage show called, *Point of No Return,* starring Henry Fonda. We paid for general admission but, once inside, quietly moved to better, unoccupied seats. As the movie started a voice suddenly commanded, "Tickets, please." We jumped in our seats! On stage, Henry Fonda looked up from his train seat at the conductor who had just approached. Whew, that was close!

One of my friends at the Topaz Internment Camp was a teenage Nisei like me named Kittee

Tsuzuki. I'd heard that she and her parents had relocated to New York City so one weekend I looked them up and enjoyed a grand reunion followed by many frequent visits. Her father was an artist and Mrs. Tsuzuki was a seamstress who made many costumes for the Olympic ice skater, Sonja Henie. Kittee was a college student. The Tsuzuki family treated me like family and later at my wedding, Kittee was one of my attendants and her father "gave me away."

An event sponsored by the New York JACL (Japanese American Citizens League) was the first social I attended upon my arrival in New York. It was a friendly gathering of many Japanese Americans like me who were new to the city and eager to make new friends. Among the many I met was Shig Kariya, a struggling businessman who impressed me with his quiet and mature demeanor. Four years earlier, in the summer of 1946, Shig was approached by a successful Japanese-American entrepreneur, George Aratani, who wanted to start a trading business with Japan. George's father was a prominent lettuce grower in Guadalupe, California. Word had it that senior Aratani set the price of lettuce for the entire country. His son wished to go into some form of business but not farming. Japan was slowly recovering from a devastating war and focusing on rebuilding itself. Both Shig and George were struggling to start new lives after years of internment camps imprisonment. During the war, George attended a U.S. military intelligence school, became an instructor, and later served in the Military Intelligence

Service. Shig, born in Japan and ineligible for citizenship at the time, was in an internment camp in Poston, Arizona. After being released, he found a job at the Donnelly Printing Company in Chicago. George's goal of building a trading company was no easy task.

As Shig and George discussed ideas and possibilities they both agreed to try importing chinaware made in Japan. Nagoya, a large industrial city in southern Honshu, had been the pottery and chinaware capital of Japan but was flattened by the relentless U.S. air bombing campaign. Shig, who was born in Nagoya City, had close relatives still in the chinaware business, and George's family had financial means. So they, Shig and George, co-founded American Commercial, Inc., which was later re-named Mikasa China. Shig traveled back to Nagoya and met with a cousin whose factory had been reduced to rubble. They envisioned a rebuilt chinaware factory whose products would be sold by retailing giants Macy's and Gimbels of New York. Years of planning, painstakingly rebuilding, endless government bureaucracy, training of craftsmen and endless travel between New York and Nagoya followed. The early days of American Commercial were touch and go; survival was never certain. It was in those precarious days that I had met Shig.

He spent much of those years traveling to/from Japan but we dated whenever he was in town. Though he was ten years my senior, we found we had much in common; we both grew up bi-culturally, were bilingual, and thought alike politically. We enjoyed movies and traveling. After eight months of dating, Shig proposed

and I accepted. We were married on June 14, 1952 at the famed Riverside Church in New York City. I borrowed my girlfriend Muriel Onishi's wedding gown which she air mailed from Honolulu. My sister Yone and Kittee were my attendants and Kittee's father, Mr. Tsuzuki, escorted me down the aisle. My parents, unfortunately, could not make it to the wedding. It was wonderful to see all my friends at the Watson Lab attend. A buffet reception followed at Columbia University's Butler Hall. We enjoyed a weekend honeymoon in the nearby Pocono Mountains in Delaware.

Shortly after we were married, we found an attractive brick house in Leonia, New Jersey across the Hudson River, just a few miles from the George Washington Bridge. Shig could not

own property as he wasn't yet a US citizen. So we bought the house under my name. Leonia was to be our home for the next forty years. Both Shig and I commuted from Leonia to our jobs in the city; I, to the Watson Lab and he, to the small offices of ACI. Two years later I retired from IBM, the company that had been so good to me to start a family, a common practice for women in those days.

Shig was the only child of Risaburo and Masa Kariya. His father, Risaburo, owned a Japanese art goods trading store in Los Angeles. Risaburo had done well in retail and his family lived in relative wealth. Alas, he died of a heart attack when Shig was four. Shig's mother, Masa, was a beautiful woman from Nagoya who took great pride in her only son. She hired a young student from Japan, Mr. Suehiro, as her son's live-in tutor, mentor and companion. Mother Kariya's family was among the Japanese wealthy and elite, and her contacts proved invaluable when Shig went into the chinaware business.

When at age 35, he told his mother he was ready to marry she looked into my background. She wasn't thrilled to discover my family was of modest means, if not exactly poor. However, we were "respectable." She ultimately gave our wedding her approval but until her death she let me know in subtle and unsubtle ways that I wasn't the equal of her son.

It was Shig's greatest desire to father three sons. Having seen my own mother manage to produce only one boy after three girls, it was an exceedingly tall order.

Amazingly, he got his wish. Steven Toshihiro was born on May 18, 1954, Scott Tatsuo on December 25, 1955 and Kent Sei on August 11, 1959. Three boys in a row.

Why, you're quite welcome, Shig! Did I wish for a daughter? In my opinion, the children's health was much more important than their gender. Anyway, I already knew what it was like to grow up with girls.

The transition from career woman to a full-time mother was relatively smooth for me. I felt blessed to have had a wonderful career but looked forward to raising a loving family. What more could a girl ask for? Being mentally stimulated, genuinely contented and born with healthy genes I worked from dawn to dusk to raise our three sons. As was common in those days, Shig came from the old school where the husband was 'Lord and Master' of his manor. Rearing kids was women's work; he never changed diaper, not even once. (A generation later, however, he tried changing his infant grandson's diaper but by that time he was too old and slow and little Michael wriggled away.) I understood and accepted his male superior Japanese upbringing. After all, I was brought up with the same notions. And his mother seemed always at hand to enforce the old traditions, i.e. wife equals silent maid/housekeeper/mother. Her son was the royal prince and she, the queen mother. Whenever I disagreed (mostly, I just kept quiet), it was no use arguing with her. When necessary, I asked Shig to intervene.

Starting a business consumes most entrepreneurs' lives and that's how it was with Shig. In addition, he needed to be in Japan a good part of the year. So, the task of raising three sons became my sole responsibility. For all practical purposes I was a single parent. For many years, Shig was rarely around and Dr. Spock became my sole source when I needed guidance. Once when we were putting an addition onto the house the contractor said to four year-old Scotty, "Your daddy is never home. You probably don't know he looks like." Scotty replied, "Oh yes I do, we have pictures of him!" Hearing this, I didn't know whether to laugh or cry.

The boys were virtually the only Asians attending Leonia public schools at that time. But, we were happily assimilated in this all-white community but Shig and I felt it was important that the boys not lose connections to their heritage. So every Saturday morning I drove them into New York City to take Japanese language and judo lessons at a

Buddhist church. Kent turned out to be an outstanding athlete and at age 13 won the national judo championship held in Odessa, Texas. Shig, himself a black belt in judo in his youth, was ecstatic. He had arranged to be home and flew with the boys to Texas to cheer them on in the national tournament. Kent's first place win was certainly a proud moment for Shig and he talked about it for days.

When Steve was accepted at Harvard I sent a telegram to Shig in Nagoya, Japan. Heretofore, I never wrote or telephoned him. The people in Japan were very concerned about Shig receiving the wire thinking some emergency had occurred. So Shig showed them the message: STEVE ACCEPTED AT HARVARD.

Scott showed an early interest in Computing. He spent hours outside of class working on a computer terminal linked to some gigantic mainframe computer at Columbia University, an early version of cloud computing. He enjoyed music and was a bugler for The Muchachos, a local drum and bugle corps (like a marching band) which traveled to competitions across the country. In his junior year Scott became the drum major for the Leonia High School marching band, and, in his senior year, became Student Body President. Upon Scott's graduation I sent a second wire to Shig in Nagoya, Japan: SCOTT ACCEPTED AT YALE.

Although Kent was a natural athlete, he struggled through middle school with mediocre grades. In the summer of 1974, we "encouraged" him to attend summer school at Choate Academy in Wallingford,

Connecticut and much to our surprise, he enjoyed it. Steve and Scott also had some prep school experience as they attended Exeter Academy's summer sessions in '73 and '74 respectively. So for his junior and senior high school years Kent studied at Choate and completed his secondary education there. After graduation, he applied to and was accepted by Boston College. Shig had curtailed his business trip to Japan considerably and was home when Kent received his acceptance letter, so we saved the price of a telegram for our last son. Alas, he petered out at Boston College after two years and moved to California to "experience life" and had a series of menial jobs. He finally came home and graduated from Pace College in Manhattan. A decade or so later, he became a middle school teacher and earned a Master's Degree in Education from Johns Hopkins. As a mother of three, I raised two early bloomers and one late bloomer. [Note to other mothers: Never give up.]

Putting three sons through college, particularly Ivy League ones, is dreadfully expensive (less so in those days but still daunting) and we did it with none of the kids receiving financial aid. Shig's salary made us comfortable, though hardly wealthy. So, how did we afford to pay for our three sons? Remember that I enrolled in the IBM stock purchase program when I began working for them in Tokyo. Luckily for us, IBM stock turned out to be one of the investment wonders of those decades. It grew and split, then did it again and again and again. I can say that the boys were schooled "on IBM scholarship."

As each of the boys left for college, my need to be at home for them grew smaller. So, when Scott left for New Haven leaving Kent as the last child at home, Shig lifted my "grounded at home responsibility" and I began to pursue more and more activities outside the house.

I took lessons in ikebana (the Japanese art of flower arrangement). Whenever the ikebana teacher got a job assignment and needed assistance I volunteered. She had frequent jobs at the Japanese Embassy in Manhattan to decorate their public areas with large and beautiful arrangements; I assisted on many of them. By this time Mikasa China, was growing and enjoyed a high profile so Shig and I were frequently invited to the Embassy as representatives of the local Japanese-American community. I remember that the BBC's production of *Upstairs, Downstairs,* contrasting the lives of English gentry with those of their servants, was all the rage then. I had my own little *Upstairs, Downstairs.* When working on the flowers at the Embassy we used the 'downstairs' (service) entrance. Later in the evening, Shig and I would arrive as guests for an Embassy party and we would be welcomed through the main 'upstairs' door. I guess I was one of the few guests who "wore two hats".

Through the recommendation of a distinguished Japanese friend, I joined the Nichibei Fujinkai (Japanese American Women's Club) a subsidiary of the Japan

Society. The club has an elite membership. Its first president was Mrs. John D. Rockefeller. In 1989 when I was president, a significant event occurred. The Metropolitan Museum received an  unusually large sliding screen dating back to the 15th century from the early days of the Ryoanji Temple in Kyoto, Japan. Like many artifacts, it needed substantial restoration costing a small fortune. The Met contacted the then ambassador's wife, Mme Hanabusa, and she asked me to serve as her Advisor/Coordinator. We raised $50,000 from an elegant event "Breakfast at Tiffany" in June 1991 which was sponsored by the Tiffany Company itself. The reconditioned elegant screen is now part of the permanent collection at The Met.

Shortly after my presidency at Nichibei, I was  invited to join the Board of the United Nations Children's Fund (UNICEF) of New York. It was my first experience of working side by side with civic notables and I felt deeply honored. UNICEF is heavily involved in humanitarian service globally. UNICEF's world ambassador then was actress Audrey Hepburn, who attended our meetings. She was indeed a gracious and dedicated volunteer and I was absolutely thrilled to meet and work with her.

I had been on the board for a few months, when I was asked to chair the annual *Nutcracker Suite* ballet fundraiser at Lincoln Center. My choice for the Honorary Chair was Japanese United Nation Ambassador Kikuchi. All our communication was in very formal Japanese which I could speak thanks to Mama who had wisely taught it to her children. Japanese companies in the U.S. were flourishing in those days but few Japanese participated in civic affairs, particularly in New York. At an early meeting, he handed me his personal check for $1,000 to kick-off the fundraising. On another visit, he waved a congratulatory letter from the then New York Mayor Ed Koch thanking him and the Japanese community for participating in civic affairs. At the ambassador's urging many of the most prominent Japanese companies donated generously to the event. Remarkably, this particular event surpassed every past UNICEF *Nutcracker* fundraising. We had all worked hard and felt proud. Moreover, I personally relished the warm camaraderie I felt among my peers.

After years of hard work, Mikasa China was finally becoming a household name. To compete against established competitors like elegant and expensive Noritake, Mikasa had to come up with pleasing artistic designs, bold and fresh ideas and new approaches to dinnerware. The company brought in chinaware designers from Nagoya to study American lifestyles. The designers abandoned their cultural conservativeness and created light and free-flowing designs. These patterns appealed to Americans of all ages and sales skyrocketed. Despite Mikasa's success, Shig never encouraged our sons to work there. He always said it was a tough business.

Steve graduated Harvard with honors and also won the prestigious "Ames Award" named for two brothers, both Harvard students, who gave their lives to save their father. He then went on to Cornell Medical College in Manhattan. In March of 1980, as a fourth year medical student, he and eight colleagues volunteered to work at a U.N. refugee camp for Cambodian refugees in Thailand. They spent four months treating patients in primitive hospital tents. He wrote to us regularly via air letters describing poor conditions and unendurable heat. We at home felt helpless but I made up a CARE package of simple goodies, i.e. Fig Newtons, Oreo cookies, candy bars, etc. packed them into a large box and sent it via airmail. The postage alone was over $200 but the thank you's that followed were well worth it.

Scott seemed interested in becoming a lawyer when he was in high school but didn't do particularly well at academically challenging Yale. While a freshman, Scott took on three jobs outside of his studies: bartending, newsstand assistant and answering a suicide 'hot line.' I pointed out to Scott that his main job was his studies, which he assured me was under control. I remember asking him, "At 17, what makes you feel you can handle the 'hot lines'" and his retort was "All you need to do is to be a good listener." After graduating, he worked for a major law firm in New York City to determine if he would like a legal career. He soon found out that it wasn't right for him. After a year working for Johnson & Johnson in New Jersey, he applied to IBM, after hearing me praise the company so often. He moved to Manhattan and worked there for five years. He eventually became a successful headhunter finding technology experts for large companies. I once told a friend that my second son was a headhunter and she looked puzzled and asked, "Scott works in Africa?" To which I replied, "No. He works in the jungle of Wall Street."

Our parents, my parents and Shig's mother, died during the boys' growing up years. My mother, Kane Hirawaki Ito, died of stomach cancer at age 59 in 1955. My sister Yone, after completing her college education in the States, had gone back to Japan and worked as a teacher at the American School in Tokyo. She and Papa took great care of Mama during her illness. Sadly, I was unable to visit Mama as I was pregnant with Scott, who was born on Christmas day that year.

Shig's mother, who asked to be called Nana, lived with us during her final years. Shig was grateful and dutiful to his strong-willed mother but at times felt smothered (as did I). As she grew frail, bedridden and sickly, I tended to her, bathed her daily and fed her. In October 1973 at age 83 she succumbed to TB and pneumonia.

In 1990 at the hearty age of 93 Papa died of the hardening of the arteries. My cousin Kiye, who took wonderful care of Papa, telephoned me from Yokohama saying Papa was in bed for three days. Papa never was sick so this was alarming news. I immediately booked a flight to Japan. He was happy to see me and talked on and on about the good ole days. His doctor was amazed at his energy and he thought he had misdiagnosed Papa but he quickly weakened  and slumbered to his death. In typical Japanese style, the mortician came to the house, bathed him, dressed him, then hung purple cloths throughout the main room. Relatives from far and near plus the neighbors came to mourn his passing. At the crematorium, the director commented on Papa's teeth, "No cavities, not even a filling. Such a rarity!"

By this time, Steve had gone from Harvard to Cornell Medical College then back to Harvard and there met Suzanne Rogacz, a future endocrinologist. They were married in January, 1985 in the Harvard Chapel. Suzanne soon joined an endocrinology team in Virginia and Steve joined a pulmonary team in Maryland. After a few years of settling, Suzanne took a short leave of absence and gave birth to Christine Mari in 1987. Two years later, in 1989 , she gave birth to Michael Hiro.

Shig had now cut back on his travel to Japan. He still worked long hours for Mikasa in New York, but now had time to participate in civic affairs mostly in the Japanese community. He served as president of the

New York Japanese American Association. In 1988, he received the prestigious Emperor's Award Fifth Order for building harmonious ties between the United States and Japan.

In 1985 Shig, together with other senior executives, retired from Mikasa through a leverage buyout. All our sons had left home. It was now time for us to enjoy traveling while we were in good health. We toured Europe, the Orient, South America and the States. During the winter we enjoyed

Hawaii and visited Japan often.

Our big 7-bedroom house was now too big. But, where to live? Staying in the New York area seemed too costly. Many of our retiring neighbors and friends had moved to either Florida or California. We were in a quandary until Steve encouraged us to move south to the Washington, DC area to be near them and help care for their children. Reciprocally, he and Suzanne, both doctors, would care for us in our old age. It all made sense, so after nearly 40 years, we left Leonia and moved into a townhouse in North Bethesda, Maryland.

Chapter V

Washington, DC

Shig's retirement began a new chapter in our lives. The decision to relocate to the Washington area fit in nicely with our overall plans. We accepted Steve's invitation to be near him and his young family; to move a wee bit south where the winter would be less severe; and to be in the culturally rich capital of America. So in 1991, we made our exodus to Bethesda, Maryland.

We had no problem selling our home in Leonia. Since we were downsizing from a 7-bedroom home to a 3-bedroom townhouse, we left most of our furniture and all our garden equipment. The new owner was delighted with the extras and I looked forward to decorating our new townhouse. The townhouse sat on land that was once the seven-acre Shriver estate/farm and since converted into a large development with houses, townhouses and condominiums. Surprisingly, it didn't take us long to feel at home in the Bethesda area. The weather is mild though the summers can get uncomfortably hot. Nearby Washington is a beautiful city with many free museums, memorials and parks. We picked a spot conveniently located near major roadways, the Metro system, shopping areas and friendly neighbors; an ideal situation for us.

Many of my friends warned me that men have a difficult time adjusting to retirement. Shig was no exception. Up until then, he ruled in his office while home was my domain. But now, we both were at home all the time, and in a much smaller home. I still ran the household, did errands, went shopping and met friends for lunch. Shig did none of that. He occupied himself in the morning by reading **The New York Times**, **Wall Street Journal**, **Washington Post**, and magazines, as well as, managing his stock portfolios. His devotion to work kept him from developing hobbies, save a little golf, so devoid of hobbies and interests he mostly puttered around, bored and lost. I encouraged him to join the YMCA or form a club with like-minded friends but to no avail. Since we both enjoyed travelling we focused on taking trips.

At about this time, we were introduced to the PANA (Pan American Nikkei Association) conferences held biennially. The purpose is for Nikkei's (people of Japanese ancestry) living in the Western Hemisphere – Canada, United States, Central America, and South America to meet socially and exchange experiences, as well as, appreciate our shared Japanese culture. The first PANA conference we attended was in 1995 in Sao Paulo, Brazil. Meetings and events were conducted in Japanese, English, Spanish and Portuguese with simultaneous translations. Since then, we attended a few more conferences held in Mexico, Argentine and Peru. (The most recent PANA conference now renamed COPANI was held in Cancun in Sept 2011 which I attended. It had a total of 285 visiting attendees (not including local participants) from 17 countries of which 35 attendees were from the United States.)

In addition to our South American trips, we also visited the Orient, Europe and the States. Vacationing in Hawaii during the winter months was especially pleasurable and visiting Japan every other year was high priority as we both had relatives and friends there.

Since Steve and Suzanne had hired a live-in nanny there was little baby sitting job for us. But when there was a need we thoroughly enjoyed caring for our little grandchildren. One day, we were asked to babysit Michael. Tina was in nursery school and I had a medical appointment so Shig took on the job alone. When I returned from the doctor's appointment hours later, I opened the door and was aghast at Shig's face. It was entirely colored in felt pen. Shig sheepishly confessed that after chasing Michael around he was so tired he sat down and must have zonked out. And, little Michael, seeing Grandpa sleeping with a clean face decided it needed some coloring. It took a lot scrubbing to clean Shig's face – days, in fact.

We were invited to join Steve and Suzanne for dinner often. Suzanne is a wonderful cook having inherited her talent from her grandfather who was a French chef. We were happily adjusting to our new life in Maryland.

Scott lived near the Jersey Shore before settling down in a comfortable apartment in Chelsea (mid-Manhattan). He enjoyed his bachelor living and cheerfully put us up whenever we went back to visit New York City. Kent lived in San Francisco for a few years and got married there, but after it soured he moved back east. He purchased a small bungalow in Bethesda near us and worked long hours in the real estate business. In 2000 Kent met and married Julia Eline, a nurse practitioner, whom Shig and I both loved. We were elated to have all three sons living in the east and two close to us in Bethesda.

I soon joined the Washington Tokyo Women's Club, whose goal is to promote friendship between the U.S. and Japan - very similar to New York's Nichibei Fujinkai. I served as hospitality chairperson, vice president and finally president in 1993. There, I had the pleasure of working closely with the Japanese ambassador's wife, Mrs. Mimi Kuriyama. We worked together when she was head of the Washington National Cathedral's Flower Mart and again assisted her in the 1993 Kobe Earthquake Relief Program.

To celebrate Shig's 80th birthday in April 1995, the boys and I hosted a special party which turned out to be a grand event. Steve and Suzanne had just  purchased a large home in nearby Potomac and during the pre-furnished period, we invited 100 guests. In addition to the usual catered food, we hired a top, local sushi restaurant. They actually erected a Japanese-gabled kiosk in the living room and served made-to-order sushi from a window to a long line of people. Guests included our newly-made local friends plus our many New York friends who stayed at a nearby hotel as our guests. The top Japanese diplomat in Washington, Ambassador and Mme. Kuriyama surprised us by accepting our invitation. There were other luminaries among the Japanese elite who came and the quiet street where Steve and Suzanne lived had more than a few waiting limos and drivers that afternoon. Shig thoroughly enjoyed that party – it really was an incredible event.

One day in 1995, out of the blue, I received a phone call from Bill Marutani, a Nisei judge from Philadelphia. He was calling on behalf of the National Japanese American Memorial Foundation. This was the entity created to fulfill the 1992 Congressional authorization to build a memorial to those Nisei who had served in the military and the 120,000 Japanese-Americans who were imprisoned during WWII. Of course I knew of the Memorial – it was the biggest news of the decade for the Japanese-American community. But, what dumbfounded me was what he said next – would I consider being a member of the Foundation's board of directors? He continued speaking but I barely remember what he said as my brain was spinning. After I hung up the phone with him, I was still in a daze. After much thought and with Shig's approval, I called Bill back and accepted the position.

Because board members lived across the country, meeting were held in New York, Washington DC. Los Angeles, San Diego, San Francisco and Honolulu. Now,

I was doing the traveling, not Shig. We worked hard but were energized by the historic significance of our mission. Seven years later, the groundbreaking of the Memorial rewarded our efforts.

The Memorial to Patriotism was dedicated on November 10, 2000 with a gala banquet. It's not a building – more like an outdoor sculpture garden ringed by Japanese Cherry trees in Washington DC just a few blocks from the Capitol and Union Station. The Memorial tells the moving story of the massive wartime internment, contains inscribed reflections on liberty, freedom and democracy, and pays honor to the more than 800 Japanese-American veterans who fought not only the enemy abroad but prejudice at home. There is a reflecting pool with five large stones representing five generations of Japanese-Americans now settled in America. In the center of the Memorial stands a magnificent 14-foot bronze statue of two cranes entangled in barbed wire, desperately trying to break free. The Memorial signifies a three-fold purpose: 1) A testament to the valor and patriotism of the Japanese-American soldiers, 2) A testament to the hardship and perseverance of the interned Japanese-Americans, and

3) A reminder of the fragility of our constitutional rights and liberties in a democratic society. Every year, there is a memorial service at the site that recalls what happened, and reminding all of the importance of upholding civil and constitutional rights particularly during times of national crisis. The program ends with a Freedom Walk and has celebrated its 14th anniversary.

In the summer of 1997, we were guests of our dear friend Florence Dalton at her vacation house in the Caribbean. Shig loved abalone, a specialty there and ate it, feasted really, every chance he had. But on this trip he came down with severe abdominal pains and became so sick that he needed a wheelchair to return home. It turned out not to be food poisoning but something far worse. He improved somewhat over the next month but soon experienced a mild stroke. In the following two years his health worsened dramatically and he was eventually hospitalized. Dr. Steve proved to be not only a loving son but a dedicated physician. While at Holy Cross Hospital where Steve worked, his many co-workers, associates, staff workers and friends visited Shig and relayed countless stories of Steve's kindnesses to them. Although dreadfully sick, Shig couldn't have been prouder; it was the best gift a parent could receive. But it wasn't enough. In spite of superb treatment and care, he succumbed on June 25, 1999.

Funeral services were held in Maryland and a week later in New York City where we lived for nearly 40 years. Shig and I had been married for 47 blessed years. Family and friends were the source of great strength and comfort to me during those difficult months as I prepared to face a new chapter in my life without him.

To fight loneliness I took advantage of the many attractions that tourists come from all over the globe to see. I visited many museums, attended lectures and soon joined several clubs. One organization, the Capital Speakers Club of Washington, D.C, helps women speak more effectively in public, similar to the Toastmaster Club. I made many friends and learned skills that would later become valuable for service work I would later do.

The Smithsonian, a staple on any D.C. tourist's list, is not one museum but 18 world-class institutions. The Freer and Sackler Galleries comprise the Smithsonian's Asian Art museums and I decided to volunteer there as a docent. There are always impressive displays but my favorite exhibition was on the Silk Road – a historic network of trade routes spanning 4,000 miles and connecting China with Europe, Africa, India and Southeast Asia. Its history goes back two thousand years. Becoming a docent there entails a lot of study and hard work – you must be knowledgeable in your subjects. I volunteered for several years but eventually left the program. I've kept my ties with Sackler/Freer by joining Friends, the gallery's support group.

Washington is, of course, a political town and I had some brief exposure to that world. At the start of Bill Clinton's second term, I became a volunteer calligrapher in the Greetings Office of The White

House drawing on my childhood classes in Japanese calligraphy. I served in that capacity for ten years running into President George W. Bush's first term. I thoroughly enjoyed working with volunteers of varied backgrounds, from generals' and admirals' wives to housewives like me. I had the opportunity to work at special events like the annual Easter Egg Hunt and attend the Volunteers' Christmas Party hosted by the First Lady. Immediately following 9/11, a photograph of President Bush shaking my hand at the White House made TV and papers around the world when he visited us volunteers and commended us for our service.

I did various volunteer stints and one of my favorite experiences was teaching Japanese language and culture to pre-teenage students at the Great Falls Elementary School's Japanese Immersion Program. One of the students' favorite culture program was celebrating the Japanese Doll Festival (March 3rd). The students wore colorful kimonos and enjoyed eating Japanese delicacies. One year, I hand quilted a large Doll Festival wall hanging (30" x 36") and presented it to  the school. However, after 15 rewarding years, the program came to an end due to changing curriculum scheduling.

In addition to my volunteer work, I have engaged in many hobbies, like needlework (counted cross stitch), painting, golfing, bridge playing, and handicraft (covering eggs with Japanese *washi* paper). Most Sunday mornings I enjoy strolling the grounds of the lush Brookside Gardens in nearby Wheaton – it's my scaled-down version of Kykuit, the Rockefeller family's estate in Westchester County in NY.

With the Memorial built, I resigned from the National Japanese American Memorial Foundation as a board member. However, I wanted to keep the story of the internment and its lessons about freedom and liberty alive in other ways. Years ago I was asked to relate my internment experience to students at a local high school. I did and was very gratified with the amazed reactions of the students who had not known of the injustice beforehand. Since that time, I have visited scores of schools

From **Bullis Magazine**, Summer 2007

Junior Michael Kariya's grandmother, Jean, spoke about her family's experiences in a Japanese internment camp during WWII.

She shared with the students how the Japanese families were notified of their dramatic change in status and her inital impressions of the first internment camp where all five members of her family were housed in a single horse stall at a south San Francisco race track.

Words from her father's weekly letters became her life's mantra: "Be strong in mind, body and spirit."

and spoken to hundreds of school children about my WWII experience in internment camps. Until the 1960's, U.S. history textbooks made no mention of the WWII treatment of Japanese-Americans. Now, many include the internment as a footnote or anecdote and teachers use it to provoke discussion about civil liberties. Most students are surprised to hear about my steadfast belief in the U.S.'s commitment to liberty and freedom despite being interned for three years. Some asked why we didn't object or fight back.. I don't have all the answers; I just tell my story. But, I believe that seeing and hearing me in person brings that piece of history alive and helps spur discussion and recognition of fundamental values we hold as Americans.

At the 2010 Cherry Blossom Freedom Walk, three of us Niseis were panel members and spoke of our WWII experiences. We were told to make our presentations short – relate a three-year experience in five minutes. I told my story which was recorded and can be found on YouTube. Shortly thereafter, I was approached to give the same speech in Japanese to a Japanese Saturday School assembly. I didn't think my Japanese, adequate for conversation, was good enough for a speech. But then I recalled the hardship my parents endured so that I would learn Japanese. I accepted the challenge and dedicated the talk to them. It took many hours and help from friends to prepare. I spoke in *nihongo* (Japanese) for fifteen minutes. It was well received. In fact, a few parents in the back gave me a standing ovation.

I believe Mama and Papa would have been pleased.

At this writing, Tina is now a 4th year medical  student majoring in Surgery at the University of Maryland. She graduated from Duke University with honors majoring in Biomedical Engineering. Michael graduated from Vanderbilt University with a major in Mechanical Engineering. Additionally, he plans to study Electrical Engineering to qualify as a Missile Engineer. My third grandchild Kiyo is in elementary school. She does well  academically and excels in sports so her future looks bright. We enjoy family reunions often like family birthdays, holidays, graduations to which Scott travels from New York to join us.

Finally, I cannot end this without thanking my wonderful three sons, Steve, Scott and Kent, their families, and all my dear friends who have been such marvelous support in my everyday living.

Acknowledgements

I'm so grateful for all the help and support I received while writing **Papa Said "Be Strong"** I'd like to express my sincere appreciation to:

Heidi Hemming, for encouraging and supporting me, and editing my manuscript from beginning to end.

Elizabeth Wix, for adding many polishing touches with her professionalism.

My son, Scott Kariya, for his encouragement and patience and finalizing the book to its publication.

I also want to express my profound appreciation to my family for their loving kindness and support especially during my last 15 years since my husband, Shig, died.

My eldest son, Steve and his wife, Suzanne, their daughter, Tina, and son, Michael.

My middle son, Scott, and his partner, Rob, and their Airedale terrier, Bodhi.

My youngest son, Kent, and his wife, Julia, daughter Kiyo, and their black Lab, Caroline.